T0146920

GOD'S
MYSTERIES
REVEALED

(DEUT. 29:29)

These Mysteries Where First Given to the Apostle Paul

William Maynard

Order this book online at www.trafford.com
or email orders@trafford.com

Most Trafford titles are also available at major online book retailers.

All scriptures given are from the King James Version of the Bible.

Printed in the United States of America.

ISBN: 978-1-4907-0539-2 (sc)
ISBN: 978-1-4907-0540-8 (e)

Trafford rev. 08/30/2013

 www.trafford.com

North America & international
toll-free: 1 888 232 4444 (USA & Canada)
fax: 812 355 4082

God's revelation is progressive in His dealings with mankind, in various ways and at various times. Since the days of Jesus' visitation, He's been dealing with mankind's soul in Love, through Faith's receptivity of Grace and Truth. It is our prayer that through the progression of this book and those to follow, all who read it will also receive His revelation. Remember this one thing concerning the book, that the revelation is constantly progressive. And that we are all continually growing in Grace and Knowledge of God and the Lord, Christ Jesus.

CONTENTS

Introduction.. ix

A Word From Glenda... 1

Faith Working Through Love... 4

Knowledge of The Mysteries.. 13

Genesis: The Untold Story... 32

Are You So Blind That You Cannot See? 57

Israel's Blindness Which Leads to Blindness of The Church.... 64

Subtle Deception of the Worldly Kind.......................... 97

Speaking the Wisdom of God in Mysteries 102

The Knowledge of God's Plan........ .,,........................ 130

True Praise 159

Introduction

THE EYE ONLY SEES WHAT THE BRAIN IS PROGRAMED TO COMPREHEND

Inattentional Blindness

"Inattentional blindness is the failure to notice an unexpected stimulus that is in one's field of vision when other attention-demanding tasks are being performed. It is categorized as an attentional error and is not associated with any vision deficits. This typically happens because humans are overloaded with stimuli, and it is impossible to pay attention to all stimuli in one's environment. This is due to the fact that they are unaware of the unattended stimuli. Inattentional blindness also has an effect on people's perception. There have been multiple experiments performed that demonstrate this phenomenon." **Most, Steven B. (2010). "What's "inattentional" about inattentional blindness?".** *Consciousness and Cognition* **19 (4): 1102. doi:10.1016/j. concog.2010.01.011 Taken from Wikipedia online.**

I recently watched a television program concerning this subject; inattentional blindness. It spoke volumes to me. Then I saw it from a spiritual point of view.

Many times we miss seeing things because our mind is on something else and focused on other things. We drive down the road talking on our phones or just listening to a song on the radio and before we know it, we are involved in an accident and swear up and down that we did not see that other car, it just wasn't there! Or something can happen right before our eyes and we don't see it at all. It can be rather unsettling at times.

There is an experiment that is done to prove this actually happens. A man is walking down the street, a beautiful young woman comes up to him to ask directions. While looking at the map she hands him, two men carrying a large board (such as plywood) cross between the man and woman. Another woman takes the first woman's place, wearing totally different clothes, different color hair, ect . . . but the man, even though he looks right at her, does not see the change.

Our eyes will only see what our brain is prepared to comprehend. When we, as children are trained or prepared for certain things in life we expect and see only that which has been instilled in us. Then someone comes along with something else, we balk at it by saying that it's not true, or it's in error or whatever.

This is what happened to Israel in their rebellion. They had been given the Law by Moses and for many generations they were prepared by and instilled with the rituals and traditions of the Law. What they didn't see or understand was that they were being kept in a corral of sorts as protection from the rest of the nations, so they wouldn't get involved in the paganism of those nations. This was to keep a pure line for the Messiah to come through. They heard the Prophets giving the word of God, but were still so focused on the Law and traditions that when the Messiah showed up, they rejected Him.

The prophesies spoke of this rejection but they didn't hear that either, because their ears were hearing only what they were prepared to comprehend as well. This is why Jesus Christ told them that those who have eyes to see and ears to hear and a heart to understand, will know that He is The Christ, the Promised Messiah.

In today's teachings we still have this inattentional blindness. Preachers preach but nobody hears, they read the Bible but nobody sees. Their minds and hearts are prepared to receive only that which they have been conditioned to receive and nothing more. Over the years they all have become "dull of seeing and hearing" as is spoken of in Deuteronomy 34:7 ***"And Moses was a hundred and twenty years old when he died: his eye was not dim, nor his natural force abated."*** Of course this is referring to Moses' physical condition, but it also stands for his spiritual condition.

Also in the words of Christ Himself, as seen in; Matthew 13:15 ***"For this people's heart is waxed gross, and their ears are dull of hearing, and their eyes they have closed; lest at any time they should see with their eyes, and hear with their ears, and should understand with their heart, and should be converted, and I should heal them."***

Preachers will tell their listeners that there is no way to understand the mysteries of God because they are "mysterious" indeed. We see here in Deuteronomy that God intended us to know and understand them.

Deuteronomy 29:29 *"The secret things belong unto the LORD our God: but those things which are revealed belong unto us and to our children for ever, that we may do all the words of this law."*

These "secret things" are all there in plain sight for those who "have eyes to see and ears to hear" We find this in simple language in;

1Corinthians 2:9 and 10 *"But as it is written, Eye hath not seen, nor ear heard, neither have entered into the heart of man, the things which God hath prepared for them that love him. But God hath revealed them unto us by his Spirit: for the Spirit searcheth all things, yea, the deep things of God."*

Hebrews 5:11 *Of whom we have many things to say, and hard to be uttered, seeing ye are dull of hearing.*

We are perfectly capable of receiving and understanding the secrets or mysteries of God, but . . . . only by His Spirit within us. We cannot comprehend them with our own minds because our minds are conditioned otherwise. There is no way with our physical senses to comprehend, but that's exactly what is attempted in the churches today, as was back in the time Jesus walked the earth.

This book, and those to follow, is intended to help others to know how to find the mysteries and to understand and comprehend those secrets as God intended. It is our prayer that each and every person that is drawn by God to read it arrives at this knowledge of God and the spiritual growth in Christ Jesus.

A Word From Glenda

O ne morning as I was awakening, I was thinking about this book and those to follow it, and how it has all come about. My husband, William and I both have given our witness of Christ and His working in and through us as individuals and a couple, over the years. When He told William that our ministry would be worldwide we really didn't comprehend the vastness of the world at that time. Even though he had been across the world while in the Air Force, and the availability of world travel has been with us for many many years now.

Since 2009 we have been on Facebook and have many friends from many places worldwide and it seems they are right here in our home with us each and every time we are on the internet. When this vehicle opened up to us, we saw the opportunity to spread the word, the gospel of Grace. Unfortunately, in the beginning, we went about it somewhat wrong and caused injury to many of our relationships with others. Some of whom we had just met and others we have known for years. That was not our intention. We only wanted to share everything that He had taught us, but now we know that it was not to be like that. We have asked their forgiveness and since have stopped to listen carefully to the Lord's instructions of when and where to share His Word. In other words, we stepped out in the flesh and the results were not at all good. So, from that point we stopped sharing all that we had learned realizing that not everyone is ready to receive it.

Recently we hosted our family reunion, as we do every year. I was talking with my brother and he said, "We can't see where we are until we see where we have been." He was referring to our walk with the Lord and the many things we go through in our lives with Him. I haven't been able to get that thought out of my mind since.

This book is that exactly. It's showing where we've been and where we have come to since. The depth of God's Amazing Grace and Mercy is something that as humans we just cannot fathom.

So, I ask you dear readers that as you read this book that The Lord has brought into your life, that you understand that it isn't about us or our walk with Him, but rather it's all about Christ.

One of the authors we read had this to say in one of his books;

CHRIST IS CHRISTIANITY AND CHRISTIANITY IS CHRIST!

All else is religion and works of the flesh. To truly walk in the Spirit means you do not listen to the voice of the flesh at all. It (the flesh) has to be put in it's place and that is dead! When I say dead, I mean it has no say in anything! This is a lesson we both are still learning. When my flesh wants something it's so difficult to not give in, but I must NOT give in! I must stand firm against that voice of the flesh. I still have my times of stumbling and falling down only because I am still in this body here on earth.

But the Apostle John says that when we sin (or give in to the flesh) we have an advocate, Christ Jesus. (I John 2:1)

As you grow in the Grace and Knowledge of God, remember what this book is all about, that being a progressive revelation. You should never think that you know all there is to know or that you have all the answers. The moment you begin doing that, you will come to realize that you really know nothing at all. We know some folks that have sat in the same church for many years and are at the same level of growth they were when we first met them over twenty years ago. There is no progressive revelation going on in their lives at all and it breaks my heart to see that happening. They will tell us that the pastor is so good, but they aren't growing. So how can what he teaches be so good? Keep all that in perspective as you read and study God's Word. It's the Life in the Word that causes growth, and the letter that kills.

My prayer for you is that of Paul; That the eyes or your understanding be enlightened that you receive the spirit of wisdom and revelation in the knowledge of God. May you walk worthy of Christ and all Righteousness remembering that Christ has become to us our wisdom, righteousness, sanctification and redemption.

I pray salvation come to you and your household and the God of Peace be with you always.

In Christ,
Glenda Maynard

FAITH WORKING THROUGH LOVE

John the Baptist, so named, because he baptized Jews into repentance and they confessed their sins. Jesus had just begun to come on the scene. In fact, Jesus had John baptize Him, because He was a Jewish man, and the Son of God it was only right that He go through it as well, but most importantly to fulfill all righteousness. This all took place before His death, burial and resurrection. His work was not finished yet, as it was just about to begin.

After Jesus was crucified, buried and rose again, before He ascended to heaven to sit at the right hand of the Father, He told His disciples to wait in Jerusalem until they be endued with power from on high. They (the 120 in the upper room) received the outpouring, or baptism, of the Holy Spirit. You can read about this in Acts 2. Then in Acts 10, Peter is told to go to Cornelius, a gentile. At that time the Holy Spirit was poured out on the gentiles. There are only two times in scripture that this happens. Why? The first time was to the Jew, then the Gentile. Paul went to the Jew first then to the gentile, when he began his ministry.

In Acts 19: 1-8 Paul had met up with some disciples on his way through the upper country to Ephesus. He asked them if they had received the Holy Spirit when they believed. They responded

4

by saying that they had never heard there was a Holy Spirit. When asked into whose baptism they had been baptized, they told him, "into John's baptism." Remember, John's baptism was only confession of sin and repentance. Then Paul laid his hands on them and they received and began to speak in tongues and magnify God.

Back in 1985, when we came into a deeper relationship with our LORD, we too, had hands laid on us to receive the baptism of the Holy Spirit, and have laid hands on many others to receive as well. However, now I see how much in error that is. OH, the Holy Spirit is not in error or receiving Him. What is in error is the fact that we do not need hands laid on us to receive anything.

What we do need is to become receptive as a little child and then to simply trust God.

FAITH WORKING THROUGH LOVE
Galatians 5:16

FAITH

God gives us a measure of faith. Romans 12:3 There is nothing we have to work for, He's even gives us the faith we need . . . .

TO BELIEVE THE GOSPEL

"For I am not ashamed of the gospel, for it is the power for salvation" . . . . Romans 1:16

"Now I make known to you brethren, the gospel which I preached . . . . which you received . . . . which also you stand . . . by which also you are saved, if you hold fast the word which I preached to you, unless you believed in vain. For I delivered to you as of first importance what I also received, that Christ died for our sins according to the Scriptures, and that He was buried and that He was raised on the third day according to the Scriptures." I Corinthians 15:1-4

"That if you confess with your mouth Jesus as Lord, and believe in your heart that God raised Him from the dead, you shall be saved (what an awesome promise from God); for with the heart man believes, resulting in righteousness, and with the mouth he confesses, resulting in salvation. For the Scripture says," 'Whoever believes in Him will not be disappointed.' For there is no distinction between Jew and Greek (gentile); for the same LORD is LORD of all, abounding in riches for all who call upon Him." Romans 10: 9-12ff

This is the only salvation gospel there is for all mankind today . . . . Jew and Gentile alike have to walk through this door by faith, believing in the FINISHED WORK of Christ.

"So faith comes by hearing, and hearing by the word of Christ." Romans 10:17

That is, hearing the true utterance (life giving Spirit) of the Lord, not just someone talking.

There is only **one way** to receive this salvation, and that is . . .

By Grace through Jesus Christ

"For by grace you have been saved through faith; and that not of yourselves, it is the gift of God." Ephesians 2:8

"He saved us not on basis of deeds which we have done in righteousness, but according to His mercy, by the washing of regeneration and renewing by the Holy Spirit, whom He poured out upon us richly through Jesus Christ our Savior . . . . being justified by His grace we might become heirs according to the hope of eternal life." Titus 3: 5-7

At the very moment we believe, we then become . . . .

Sealed with the Holy Spirit

"Who also sealed us and gave us the Spirit in our hearts as a pledge." II Corinthians 1:22

"In Him, you also after listening to the message of truth, the gospel of your salvation, having also believed, you were sealed in Him with the Holy Spirit of promise." Ephesians 1:13

"And do not grieve the Holy Spirit of God, by whom you were sealed for the day of redemption." Ephesians 4:30

In this dispensation of Grace, we are not "baptized in the Holy Spirit" . . . . but rather, we are "SEALED IN HIM (CHRIST) WITH or BY THE HOLY SPIRIT"

Now that we have salvation and are sealed with the Holy Spirit we must . . . .

Seek to know Him in a deeper relationship

"For this reason . . . . having heard of the faith . . . which exists among you . . . I do not cease . . . making mention of you in my prayers . . . . that the Father of glory may give to you a spirit of wisdom and revelation in the knowledge of Him . . . . that the eyes of your understanding be enlightened so that you may know what is the hope of His calling, what are the riches of the glory of His inheritance in the saints." Ephesians 5:15-18

Or you could ask this way, "spirit of revealed wisdom in the knowledge of Him"

"Study to show thyself approved unto God, a workman that need not be ashamed, rightly dividing the word of truth." II Timothy 2:15

"Therefore, beloved, . . . be diligent to be found by Him in peace, spotless and blameless, and regard the patience of our Lord to be salvation . . . . Paul according to the wisdom given to him, wrote to you, as also in all his letters . . . some things hard to understand, which the untaught and unstable distort, as they do the rest of the scriptures to their own destruction. You, therefore, beloved, be on your guard . . . grow in the grace and knowledge of our Lord and Savior Jesus Christ." II Peter 3: 14-18

When we ask for the spirit of revealed wisdom in the knowledge of Him, the answer is always YES. If we are diligent in our seeking to know our Lord, our spiritual eyes and ears will be opened. God is Spirit and spiritually is the only way we will come to know Him, not with our mind (soul). With all this we then come to the place where we . . . .

Grow into Maturity

"For we know in part, and we prophesy in part; but when the perfect comes, the partial will be done away. When I was a child I used to speak as a child, think as a child, reason as a child; when I became a man, I did away with childish things. For now we see in a mirror dimly, but then face to face; now I know in part, but then I shall know fully just as I also have been fully known." I Corinthians 13: 9-12

"He gave some as apostles . . . . for the equipping of the saints for the work of service, to the building up of the Body of Christ . . . . attain to the unity of faith . . . and of the knowledge of the Son of God, to a mature man, to the measure of the stature which belongs to the fullness of Christ . . . . we are no longer children tossed to and fro by every wind of doctrine . . . ." Ephesians 4:11-14ff

"Therefore, leaving the elementary teaching about the Christ, let us press on to maturity, not laying again the foundation of repentance from dead works and of faith toward God." Hebrews 6:1

Once we have grown into that maturity, the fullness of Christ, then we are able to . . .

Walk by the Spirit

"But I say, walk by the Spirit and you will not carry out the desires of the flesh." Galatians 5:16 There is no more "trying to clean yourself up" or "having to behave" or "trying to make yourself do the right things", it then comes naturally.

"For all who are led by the Spirit of God, they are the sons of God." Romans 8:14

Regardless of where, how, when and yes, even in the "hard to understand" things He wants you to do.

When we come into the maturity, and even as we are growing, we can truly see then that it's not at all a "feel good" gospel. There are many hard times, but that's why He gave us His Grace. We don't always see how things are really supposed to be. We only know of what we've been told by others. That's why we must grow and not stay as children that accept anything and everything that comes along. In the mature man is the true . . . .

Operation of the Spiritual Gifts

"Now there are diversities of gifts, but the same Spirit . . . differences of administrations, but the same Lord . . . . diversities of operations, but it is the same God that works all in all. But,

the manifestation of the Spirit is given to man to profit withal." I
Corinthians 12:4-7

"And He gave some to be apostles; and some prophets; and some
evangelist; and some pastors and teachers; for the perfecting of
the saints, unto the work of ministering, unto the building up of
the Body of Christ: **till we all attain unto the unity of the faith,
and of the knowledge of the Son of God, unto a full grown
man**, unto the measure of the stature of the fullness of Christ: that
we may be no longer children, **tossed to and fro and carried
about with every wind of doctrine, by the sleight of men, in
craftiness, after the wiles of error;** but speaking the truth in
love, we may grow up in all things unto Him, who is head, even
Christ; from whom all the body fitly framed and knit together
through that which every joint supplies, according to the working
in due measure of each several part, makes the increase of the
body unto the building up of itself in love." Ephesians 4:11-17

The gifts of the Spirit are not given to us for our entertainment
and fun, but rather so we can grow thereby into that mature
man in Christ. If we are not walking by the Spirit, mature as
we should be, we have only the power of the soul in operation.
"We walk by faith and not by sight "(II Corinthians 5:7) not by
"goose bumps" or any other emotional feelings, not by seeing
angel feathers or gold dust or any other such apparitions. That's
nothing more than the flesh, which is purely entertainment. Or
possibly even apparitions of the working of Satan for deception.

We are given the gift of Grace from God through our Lord
Jesus Christ. The gifts, administrations and operations are in

that one gift. As John Wesley said in one of his commentaries on I Corinthians 12, "There are diversities of gifts, but the same Spirit-Diverse streams, but all from one fountain."

All is done in . . . .

Love

"If I speak with the tongues of men and angels, but do not have love, I have become a noisy gong or a clanging cymbal. And if I have the gift of prophecy, and know all mysteries and all knowledge; and if I have all faith so as to remove mountains, but do not have love, I am nothing. And if I give all my possessions to feed the poor, and if I deliver my body to be burned, but do not have love, it profits me nothing." I Corinthians 13: 1-3ff

KNOWLEDGE OF THE MYSTERIES

We find ourselves often in a maze of worldly confusion. If we did not have the Holy Spirit to guide us through this massive amount of unnecessary knowledge, we would take in so much and absorb nothing. Our minds are like an attic where we store things. These things consist of items that are very important and dear to our hearts, but the time comes when we begin shoving all sorts of things in there that are of no importance at all. What then happens to the important items? They are lost in a sea of junk, in which we either cannot locate them when needed or they disappear altogether. This is the way with God's Word. We have no idea how to find the mysteries because we are so busy stuffing ourselves with so knowledge that is merely historical and of no real value to our spiritual growth. The Apostles Paul and Peter both tell us to renew our minds, and to have the mind of Christ. So, we start shoving all the information we can about Jesus and His life here on earth and all the Jewish history and traditions, thinking this is what we need. Where does the Holy Spirit fit into all this? He doesn't or can't! We think we know all there is to know but we aren't allowing Him to show us what is really important!

All things spiritual start with an understanding of the first three chapters of Genesis. It is there that we learn just what it is that was lost to mankind. Genesis is the foundation upon which Christ, in all wisdom and knowledge, is first seen and known. For it is there that the first law of "ONE" is revealed which holds the key to all else in the Bible for us.

Beginning in Genesis going through to Acts 8 and a portion of 9, we find God at work with the earthy man, or non-spiritual man (This is also seen in Romans 1-5:5). Through this, He then finds those men who have been accounted by Him as righteous or spiritual, that have met His righteous requirements. Then further in Acts 9 He focuses on one man again just as He did with Moses. We know him as Paul, his name was Saul of Tarsus, a Hebrew Pharisee and lawyer. His name change was to indicate the change of direction spoken of by the Prophets of old and Christ in His ministry to Israel. Paul then became God's voice to reveal the mysteries that had been sealed up in the book. We see Paul's ministry through the majority of the book of Acts of the Apostles and his letters revealing the mysteries from Romans through Philemon and even Hebrews. Yes, I believe Paul was responsible for the letter to the Hebrew-Christians.

Those who do not understand the word, do not see or hear this change taking place because the god of this evil world has their minds blinded or veiled to it. He's filling their "attic" with so much unnecessary information making them believe they are to stick with all the physical rites, rituals and traditions. Men of the intellectual institutions do not have a clue as to what the Lord is doing; they reveal this in their mixing of the scriptures and the blending of them to get them to say something that is not there. They take all things of the word in a religiously literal sense, in the same way as idolatrous Israel, seeking knowledge only of the traditions of men. They cannot see the metaphors and veiled language hidden because they are not spiritual. Therefore they are hindered the same as with the Hebrews because this is what had happened to them. The words literal and religion are both actions that bind up or hinder God. The people of the literalistic nature that are hungry and thirsty for the truth do not know where to turn to find this Truth. Because they have oftentimes been lead astray and deceived into believing a lie as contained in a feel good gospel, a gospel in many cases that was meant for Israel only.

Before we move on, you may be wondering why we are writing and revealing these things. You may be asking also, are they really what we say they are? In answer to this, please allow me to show you in scriptures, our charge or instructions, for doing what we are here doing. This is found in 1Corinthians 4 and within the first two verses is the key word, "steward". A steward is one who is given charge of the house or family affairs under the Head of the Family, in our case this is Christ Jesus the Head of the Church, His Body. Here Paul is speaking to the young Corinthian-Christians.

1Corinthinas 4:1-5 "Let a man so account of us, as of the ministers of Christ, and **stewards of the mysteries of God. Moreover it is required in stewards, that a man be found faithful**. But with me it is a very small thing that I should be judged of you, or of man's judgment: yea, I judge not mine own self. For I know nothing by myself; yet am I not hereby justified: but He that judges me is the Lord. Therefore judge nothing before the time, until the Lord come, who both will bring to light the hidden things of darkness, and will make manifest the counsels of the hearts: and then shall every man have praise of God." (emphasis mine)

From here we'll look at what Peter has to say.

1Peter 4:1-11 "For as much then as Christ has suffered for us in the flesh, arm yourselves likewise with the same mind: for he that has suffered in the flesh has ceased from sin; **That he no longer should live the rest of his time in the flesh to the lusts of men, but to the will of God.** For the time past of our life may suffice us to have wrought the will of the Gentiles, when we walked in lasciviousness, lusts, excess of wine, revelings, banquetings, and abominable idolatries: Wherein they think it strange that we run not with them to the same excess of riot, speaking evil of us: Who shall give account to Him that is ready to judge the quick and the dead. For this cause was the gospel preached also to them that are dead, that they might be judged according to men in the flesh, but live according to God in the spirit. But the end of all things is at hand: be therefore sober, and watch unto prayer. And above all things have fervent charity among yourselves: for charity shall cover the multitude of sins. Use hospitality one to another without grudging. **As every man has received the gift, even so minister the same one to another, as good stewards of the manifold grace of God. If any man speak, let him speak as the oracles of God; if any man minister, let him do it as of the ability which God gives: that God in all things may be glorified through Jesus Christ,**

to whom be praise and dominion for ever and ever." Amen. (emphasis mine)

Within each passage of scripture we've heard that we are to be good stewards not just with the gift given but through that same gift which was given to all who are IN Christ, to minister the Grace of God to all.

I did some research sometime back on the subject of the mysteries. What I found was that within every religion, cult and sect there are those who have become a priest. These people are chosen by their peers because they possess the revelation or secrets of the magical formulas of that religion. These they hold close to their chest keeping them to themselves, because they do not reveal any of them to any one on penalty of death. This also holds true today in most of our churches. The pastors or priests want to keep their "job" so they continue to keep the congregations dependent on them and their teachings. They are in a way telling them that only certain people can hear from God and teach His word. This is a blatant lie! Your pastor may not be saying this in so many words, but have you ever asked him/her specific questions that they cannot answer? We have, and it broke our hearts that the man standing in front of his congregation did not have the answers or couldn't tell us where we might find them. What then was this man getting and from what source? What or who made him qualified to lead others and was he leading them to the Kingdom of God by Grace or to the eternal doom? What is his motivation? What is coming out of his mouth? Look at James, he tells us that the tongue is the revealer of the heart of man by what comes out of the mouth.

James 1:26 *"If any man among you seem to be religious, and bridles not his tongue, but deceives his own heart, this man's religion is vain."*

James 3:5-6, 8 *"Even so the tongue is a little member, and boasts great things. Behold, how great a matter a little fire kindles! And the tongue is a fire, a world of iniquity: so is the tongue among our members, that it defiles the whole body, and sets on fire the course of nature; and it is set on fire of hell." . . . "But the tongue can no man tame; it is an unruly evil, full of deadly poison."*

What James is saying in these scriptures is that the teachings man gives out to others is setting the fire of hell, the very wrath of God within the soul of man, if he is not approved of God and an accepted revealer or steward of THIS Gospel of Grace.

But with God it is not to be this way! He wants ALL men to know and understand ALL the secrets and in fact, as we have learned, we are to reveal them to ALL, to hold nothing back! This is our charge and our respectability to the Church the Body of Christ. Each person is to be a responsible person, adequately equipped first to Christ and then to his fellowman . . . neighbors, friends and families. Paul is emphasizing to the converts the importance of understanding God's mystery. Colossians 2:1-7

"For I want you to know how great a struggle I have for you and for those at Laodicea and for all who have not seen me face to face, that their hearts may be encouraged, being knit together in love, to reach all the riches of full assurance of **understanding and the knowledge of God's mystery, which is**

Christ, in Whom are hidden all the treasures of wisdom and knowledge. I say this in order that no one may delude* you with plausible arguments.** For though I am absent in body, yet I am with you in spirit, rejoicing to see your good order (*discipline and righteousness*) and the firmness of your faith in Christ. As you received Christ Jesus the Lord, so walk in Him, rooted and built up in Him, and established in your faith, **even as you were taught**, abounding in thanksgiving." (emphasis mine)

*   *Delude: is to deceive, beguile to turn away from, as a wife turns her back on her husband to pursue another; as Israel and the church have done by turning toward the spirit of the world. They twist and distort this Gospel.*
** *Arguments: persuasive words*

Colossians 4:2-6

"Continue steadfastly in prayer, being watchful in it with thanksgiving. At the same time, pray also for us, that God may open to us a door for the word, **to declare the mystery of Christ**, on account of which I am in prison– **that I may make it clear**, which is how I ought to speak. Walk in wisdom toward outsiders,* making the best use of the time. Let your speech always be gracious, seasoned with salt, so that you may know how you ought to answer each person." (emphasis mine)

*   *Outsiders: unbelievers and the enemies of the cross of Christ (a sinner), seeing your manner of living (conversation).*

You see in this passage of scripture that Paul tells us that we too have the responsibility to pray for those who are revealing the mysteries. That they may speak so that they are clearly understood and received in the manner in which God desires. Those giving and those receiving are to be accountable for what they give out and receive in.

Colossians 2:9-17

"For in Him dwells all the fullness of the Godhead*. And you are filled with Him, Who is the head of all principality and power. In Whom also you are circumcised with circumcision not made by hand in despoiling** of the body of the flesh: but in the circumcision of Christ. Buried with Him in baptism:*** in Whom also you are raised again by the faith of the operation of God Who has raised Him up from the dead. And you, when you were dead in your sins and the uncircumcision of your flesh, He has quickened together with Him, forgiving your all offenses: blotting out the handwriting of the decree that was against us, which was contrary to us****. And He has taken the same out of the way, fastening it to the cross. Despoiling the principalities and powers, he has exposed them confidently in open show, triumphing over them in Himself. Let no man therefore judge you in meat or in drink or in respect of a festival day or of the new moon or of the Sabbaths, which are a shadow of things to come: but the body is of Christ."

* foundation or federal head of the Body
** stripping away or destroying by the circumcision of the heart
*** this is an action of the Holy Spirit and not with water
**** that which was lost in Adam
***** the spirit of the world in the flesh of man

All those things that made up the basis of the Jewish religion and Judaism were but a shadow of the better things that they pointed towards that were to come. In effect, Paul is saying do not allow anyone to defraud you by telling you that you must adhere to certain rites, rituals and or ceremonies. These are all filled with guile, deceit and deception. Keeping in mind that when the full Light in Truth comes the shadow is gone. There is no more need to perform these duties. The gathering of those who are IN Christ to encourage, edify and strengthen each other, building up the Body of Christ is something totally different. All the churches that we have ever been to, and I say . . . that is a lot, have all done the very same things. They all perform their little rites, rituals and ceremonies while professing to be one in spirit. Not so . . . . God is Spirit and those who worship Him MUST do so in spirit and in truth! In other words, they are to have a working knowledge of the mystery of this Gospel of Grace. The performance laws of the Jews has been dispersed and destroyed, however hard they try to keep it going and are in the process of rebuilding the temple in Jerusalem, which was torn down in or around 66-70 AD. This was done to show that it was over! No more did man need to perform, he only needs to receive Christ and allow Christ to Live His Life in him. This is faith!! . . . . not that "name it and claim it", "declare and decree", "blab it and grab it", all that health, wealth and prosperity gospel which is believing for something so hard that you, yourself, in a sense, conjure it up like a magician. This fallacy is taught too much and is causing so many people to travel that broad way that is taking them on the fast track to hell fire and eternal destruction!

God wants us just as He created Adam, a divine spiritual being. Adam didn't even have a body when he was first created. God gave him a body and breathed life into it so Adam could walk around and tend the Garden created for his pleasure. When the Light and Truth, which is Christ, fills your body and soul there is no way that sickness and disease or any darkness can dwell in it. When He is living His Life in me and through me, all my needs are met without my having to beg for it. My bank account may not show thousands of dollars, but I will always have sufficiency for every need. If I get sick in my body or injured, I will go to the doctor. God is not opposed to my taking a medicine that will ease pain or clear up an infection. After all this body was made from the dust of the earth and is subject to the curse placed upon it at Adam's fall.

Ephesians 1:7-14

"In Him we have redemption through His blood, the forgiveness of our trespasses, according to the riches of His grace, which He lavished upon us, in all **wisdom and insight making known to us the mystery of His Will, according to His Purpose**, which **He set forth in Christ** as a plan for the fullness of time, **to unite all things in Him again**, things in heaven and things on earth. In Him we have obtained an inheritance, having been **predestined according to the purpose** of Him who works all things according to the **counsel of His Will**, so that we who were the first to hope in Christ might be to the praise of His glory. In Him you also, when you heard the word of truth, the gospel of your redemption, and believed in Him, were sealed with the promised Holy Spirit, who is the guarantee of our inheritance until we acquire possession of it, to the praise of His glory." (emphasis mine)

What is redemption? It is this; a restoring of Light and Life to the darkened soul and the quickening of man's spirit by being reconnected in conjunction or the conjoining with the ontological essence of Christ as it was in Genesis chapter 2. In other words, we are again created in His image and likeness. Paul says it himself that we are "new creatures" or "new creations" of this image and likeness of God. Until this happens, we are in the image and likeness of the god of this world, Satan.

Colossians 3:1-4

"If then you have been raised with Christ, seek the things that are above, where Christ is seated at the right hand of God. Set your minds on things that are above, not on things that are on earth. For you have died, and your life is hid with Christ in God. When Christ who is your life appears, then you also will appear with Him in glory."

We read but do we understand? We have eyes that see these words and ears that hear them being read, but where is the understanding of what is being revealed? These are the mysteries that we are responsible to seek the knowledge of for ourselves. Depending only on the Spirit of Truth to reveal them to us. If for some reason we see something different than others do, we had better check ourselves to see that we are hearing the right spirit. The spirit of deception will snatch you every way he can and you will not even be aware of it, and you will die in your sins.

Philippians 3:20-21

"For our citizenship is in heaven; whence also we wait for a Savior, the Lord Jesus Christ: who shall fashion anew the body of our humiliation, that it may be conformed to the body of His glory, according to the working whereby He is able even to subject all things unto Himself."

We may be here on earth, but our home has been changed to heaven, and if all we are looking for is the comfort and pleasure of the flesh here on earth, we are looking for the wrong things.

Now for the warning:

Colossians 2:8

"See to it that no one takes you captive by philosophy and empty deceit, according to human tradition, according to the elemental spirits of the world, and not according to Christ."

This warning has gone unheeded by the world's religions now for over 1700 years or so, since the prince of darkness found out that he could slip into to figure of a angel of light and counterfeit the workings of God. Why? Because human nature, under his sway, loves darkness more than the Light of Truth. It was this darkness that first rejected Jesus and sought to kill him by what ever means available at the time.

Colossians 2:18-23

"Let no one disqualify you, insisting on asceticism* and worship of angels, going on in detail about visions, puffed up without reason by his sensuous mind, and not holding fast to the Head, from whom the whole body, nourished and knit together through its joints and ligaments, grows with a growth that is from God. If with Christ you died to the elemental spirits of the world, why, as if you were still alive in the world, do you submit to regulations—"Do not handle, Do not taste, Do not touch" (referring to things that all perish as they are used)—according to human precepts and teachings? These have indeed an appearance of wisdom in promoting self-made religion and asceticism** and severity to the body, but they are of no value in stopping the indulgence of the flesh and the wrath to come."

*   *rigid self denial*
** *which is spiritual pride under the mocking guise of humility, the taking lightly this Gospel*

Christ Himself gives this warning in Matthew 23:27-28;

"Woe to you, scribes and Pharisees, hypocrites! For you are like whitewashed tombs, which outwardly appear beautiful, but within are full of dead people's bones and all uncleanness. So you also outwardly appear righteous to others, but within you are full of hypocrisy and lawlessness."

Paul continues with this warning in 2Corinthians 11:13-15;

"For such men are false apostles, deceitful workmen, disguising themselves as apostles of Christ. And no wonder, for even Satan disguises himself as an angel of light. So it is no surprise if his servants, also, disguise themselves as servants of righteousness. Their end will correspond to their deeds."

In these two verses we are told that those who speak or preach without the knowledge of Christ, the mysteries and Will of God, are nothing in the eyes of God but lawless men, false apostles, stinking inside of death and mere instruments of Satan, the greatest of all deceivers.

1 Timothy 4:3-5

"who forbid marriage and require abstinence from foods that God created to be received with thanksgiving by those who believe and know the truth. For everything created by God is good, and nothing is to be rejected if it is received with thanksgiving, for it is made holy by the word of God and prayer."

Philippians 3:18-19

"For many walk, of whom I told you often, and now tell you even weeping, that they are the enemies of the cross of Christ: whose end is perdition, whose god is the belly, and whose glory is in their shame, who mind earthly things."

"Who mind earthly things" this is the same present day message that we spoke of earlier about health, wealth and prosperity. All the while, these who preach this will attempt to make you follow specific ways of acting, foods you can or cannot eat and how to dress. All of this and more are NOT God's message for us, a message of here and now. Why? Because mankind's Redeemer has been here and has finished His appointed task and returned to the Father, until the time He returns for His Body. This Body is mostly unknown and therefore invisible to the many on the broad road to death's door and what lays just past it, hells fire as spoken before. Wherein they'll wait for the call to come forth for the judgment. When they'll receive a body doomed for eternal punishment and disgrace of rejecting the absoluteness of God's Love.

Colossians 3:5-15

"Put to death therefore what is earthly in you: sexual immorality, impurity, passion, evil desire, and covetousness, which is idolatry. On account of these the wrath of God is coming. In these you too once walked, when you were living in them. But now you must put them all away: anger, wrath, malice, slander, and obscene talk from your mouth. Do not lie to one another, seeing that you have put off the old self with its practices and have put on **the new self, which is being renewed in knowledge after the image of its creator**. Here there is not Greek and Jew, circumcised and uncircumcised, barbarian, Scythian, slave, free; but Christ is all, and in all. Put on then, as God's chosen ones, holy and beloved, compassionate hearts, kindness, humility, meekness, and patience, bearing with one another and, if one has a complaint against another, forgiving each other; as the Lord has forgiven you, so you also must forgive. Above all these put on love, which binds everything together in perfect harmony. Let the peace of Christ rule in your hearts, to which indeed you were called in one body. Be thankful."

This is telling us that Sunday or Saturday, Wednesday, Easter, Christmas, Saint Patrick's Day or any other man made holiday of worship is defilement to the true Christian and the Hebrew-Christian community of believers (if the Hebrew has renounced his Jewish heritage and turned whole heartedly to Christ). Many billions of believers have gone to their death without knowing the mystery of this Gospel of God's Grace in Truth. Because of mans own ignorance from which there is NO escape. That is why the LORD, through Paul and the others, warns us time and time again to study the scriptures for ourselves. We are accountable to no one else but to Him for our own selves and our ignorance bears on no one else. Though the blood of all that sit under such false prophets and teachers is on their hands for they carry the heavier load or weight.

We have asked the LORD just how to make His voice heard in a clear and audible tone as His words do not have a strong enough emphasis on the printed page. The printed page or text does have the shock value or emphasis needed to grab our attention as the Spoken Word. So we are resigned to the Holy Spirits teaching, to see and hear the Word the way it's meant to be seen and heard. Men preach what they see and hear, but is it what God wants proclaimed?

So what are the mysteries?

1. Mankind through The Redeemer has already been justified, made righteous and set free from the sin nature.
2. We have become heirs of God and His righteousness.
3. A blindness and further hardening of heart was imparted to Israel to complete their blindness.
4. The revelation IS Christ.
5. The wisdom of God was hidden and is to be understood by all mankind.
6. We are to be stewards of the revelation of these mysteries.
7. The mysteries are only understood in Faith.
8. It requires our being Spiritual.
9. All those in Christ are changed in nature and character.
10. They know God's Will in all wisdom.
11. They are Stewards of God's Grace to proclaim Christ's Richness received by Faith.
12. To make known this Gospel of Christ restored in us.
13. To be empowered by Grace to make plain, in simple language, the utterance of the secrets.
14. That the Church is to be the pillar and support of the Truth.

Of course as is the custom of God, He also gives us warning for rejection of His Love and disobedience of His revealed Will, His Word. These can be found in:

In Hebrews 11:7 we see that Noah, moved by trusting what he heard, in other words he accepted, received within himself this gospel and revealed it to others.

Jonah 3:1-10 Obeyed, though he first resisted.

2 Samuel 2:20-23 Ignored and death followed. (Luke 16:23-28)

Genesis 2:16-17 Rejected and brought separation from God upon all man kind there after. (Luke 16:23-28; Destruction Proverbs 29:1)

Genesis 19:14 Scoffed at by Lot's son-in-law by mocking. (judgment for, Jude 6-7, brings destruction Proverbs 29:1)

Numbers 14:40-45 Disobeyed by presumption and were destroyed. (1 Kings 13:1-26, brings destruction Proverbs 29:1)

Now, for Paul's warnings as they apply to all and especially those who profess Faith and righteousness acquired, in that faith:

Galatians 1:6-10, 5:5-10 Against another gospel.

Hebrews 2:1-4 The other gospel causes many to drift away from the Truth and our hope of Salvation.

Hebrews 3:7-4:13 How Israel failed to come into God's rest through unbelief and disobedience.

Hebrews 5:11-6:20 Against sloth and apostasy.

Hebrews 10:26-39 against sinning willfully and drawing back into religion.

Hebrews 12:14-29 To beware of sin and rejection of Christ.

This is the beginning of the revelation of the mysteries of God and our becoming a son of God through Christ and faith in Love. When we learn of Him and how we are to tap into His virtue and Salvation, we start the process of growing in His knowledge. (Matthew 11:29) Because He is revealed by progressiveness of revelation or divine illumination from within our restored heart of hearts. He builds one brick upon another as we are able to receive of Him until we are perfected but never excelling or surpassing our Master. As we pass through each room of our mansion, where He prepares a place for us, we can claim our ownership of the mansion or room, and acquire its key or keys. So I encourage you to stay the course with us in this great adventure and thereby allow Him to be God.

GENESIS: THE UNTOLD STORY

As contained in chapters 1 through 3

T he Bible, for many years, was veiled from our understanding though we spent hours reading and studying it. Like many others we traveled down this road and that road, as both the Spirit and our-self desire would lead us, looking for the key to open this book for understanding and enlightenment. We listened to many respected theologians and pastors on our quest to learn the mystery of the scriptures as we knew that there was something missing, (Philippians 3:7, 8-10; Matthew 13:44-46; Luke 14:26; Acts 20:24; Romans 8:18; Hebrews 3:14) but we did not know what exactly it was or even what we were looking for. We, like so many before us, had no idea that the Bible is written in a sort of code and that one has to be born again, spiritually awakened before its mysteries and secrets can be understood. It took the Spirit of Christ alive in us to bring about the change that changed everything, as He turned our world inside out and upside down. He threw out everything that we had learned and caused us to start all over again. To learn of, and from Him (Matthew 11:28-30, [29]; Genesis 7:23; Romans 6:14, 8:1-2, 1Corinthians 1:30; 2Corinthians 5:17; Galatians 2:20). He told us many years ago, that we would have to pass through a lot of difficult things that some people would not believe or understand and would even shake their heads at in disbelief (Psalm 78:13, 136:14; Zechariah 10:11). All we can say is, He is faithful to His word.

Once we receive the ontological essence of the Spirit of Christ, Who is all Grace and Truth (John 1:14, 17; Colossians 1:6; 2 John 1:3), we then ask, "What is grace and our duty in truth?" Grace is defined as; the benefit of the merciful kindness by which God, exerting His holy influence upon souls, turns them to Christ, keeps, strengthens, increases them in Christ's faith, knowledge, righteousness, affection, and kindles them to the exercise of Christ likeness in His virtues. The spiritual condition of one governed by the power of Divine Grace, correcting their character and natures to develop that of Gods. All the while, we must be sitting under God listening.

Truth is the answer to this in two parts and these parts run in parallel. The first is our duty to God, it is the respecting of God, and the execution of His purposes through Christ, while sitting under God listening. The second is directed toward our fellow man, who is opposing himself by, or with, the superstitions of the gentile nations and the self proposed ordinances of the Hebrews, and the corrupt opinions and precepts of false teachers even among Christians and Hebrews. Truth is defined as a personal excellence; that candor of mind which is free from affection, pretense, simulation, falsehood, and deceit.

From here then we'll look at Genesis the first three chapters:

Genesis 1:1-5

"In the beginning God created the heaven and the earth. The earth was without form, and void; and darkness was upon the face of the deep. The Spirit of God moved upon the face of the waters. God said, 'Let there be light' (Psalm 97:11; John 1:5; 2Corinthians 4:6; 1John 1:5): and there was light (Light brought life where there was no life before). God saw the light, that it was good: and God divided the light from the darkness (Ephesians 5:8)." See also: Proverbs 8:22-31; Ephesians 3:9; Colossians 1:17; Hebrews 1:10

God has many aspects and attributes which forms the trinity. God IS the Son and they (Father of spirits, and the Son) are all correct in this instance. His Hebrew name "Yehovah" means, "the ever-revealing one" or "progressively revealed" as the "I AM that I AM" of Exodus 3:14. He is ever revealing Himself to those who are receptive of Him and are willing to sit under God listening.

John 1:1-5 and verse10

"In the beginning was the Word, and the Word was with God, and the Word was God. The same was in the beginning with God. All things were made by him; and without him was not anything made that was made. In him was life; and the life was the light of men. The light shined in darkness; and the darkness comprehended it not . . . . He was in the world, and the world was made by him, and the world knew him not."

John 8:12

"Then spake Jesus again to them, saying, 'I am the light of the world: he that follows me shall not walk in darkness, but shall have the light of life.'"

John 9:4-5

"'I must work the works of him that sent me, while it is day: the night comes, when no man can work. As long as I am in the world, I am the light of the world.'"

John 12:46

"'I am come a light into the world, that whosoever believes on me should not abide in darkness.'" (Colossians 1:15-17; Ephesians1:4-6; 2:10; 4:4-7)

John 1:14,17

"The Word was made flesh, and dwelt among us, (and we beheld his glory, the glory as of the only begotten of the Father,) full of grace and truth . . . . For the law was given by Moses, but grace and truth came by Jesus Christ."

God called the light Day, and the darkness he called Night. And the evening and the morning were the first day. Day is a metaphor for the Light of the nature of God; Night is a metaphor of darkness, the nature of Satan. (Romans 1:19-21; Psalm 33:6, 9; 148:1-5) From the fall, man has the ability to serve one or the other but not both at the same time. We have freedom of choice, or the will to choose which one we serve. Remember Esau? He chose to sell his birth right because he saw no value in it. We have the same ability. If we choose to follow the ways of the world, in mans religion of reasoning, as Esau did, we in effect have sold our birth right or the redemption through which we are to pass to reach Salvation. This is the outcome that Jacob saw, but Esau lacking trust, did not. And if we sell our birth right, we could very well remain forever doomed for destruction and hell's fire. For in religion there remains no reward through repentance when repentance is repeated often. This is seen by the re-birthing (in the Christmas story) of the baby Jesus and the crucifixion (Easter story) which keeps him on the cross, although His Resurrection is celebrated, but not the ascended Lord, man's Redeemer. You may ask how is this possible? The Truth is, on both accounts, though scriptural, are but myths with hidden meanings reaching back in time, some belonging to Egypt and even before then into preflood days when fallen angels roamed freely among man. Here again, Genesis 3:15 comes into play in the enmity between man and God and then enmity between the serpent or Satan, and man. This is where man's reasoning and that of religious orders start.

Genesis 1:26-29

"God said, 'Let us make man in our image*, after our likeness'**. So God created man in his image, in the image of God created he him; male and female created he them. God blessed them and said, 'Let them have dominion over the fish of the sea, and over the fowl of the air, and over the cattle, and over all the earth, and over every creeping thing that creeps upon the earth." Genesis 3:22; 5:1; 1 Corinthians 11:7; 2Corinthians 3:18; Ephesians1:4 4:24; Colossians 3:10 (Genesis 9:2-3; James 3:7)

*   *character, a shadow of*
**   *nature of, the Hebrew means water and the Aramaic means blood; both are in movement as the water flows up the vine to the fruit and in the fruit it turns to the juice as in a grape, the blood causes the produce to resemble its parent, in similitude*

God created man as a divine spiritual being in His own image and likeness and placed him in a body made of earth as a vehicle to care for the garden. With this, He gave him the dominion over all things. All of which was taken away in the fall and is to be restored in our redemption process.

The Life force, the very Divine nature and character (Grace, Righteousness, Holiness, Justice or Justification, Agape Love) of God, each Personification of the Godhead respectively, Father, Son and Holy Spirit, becomes ONE with man, so man then becomes a mirror image of his Creator. The Grace of God is Christ in this new creation of man. A spirit being in which are life, love, and light living in the covering of glory and the Kingdom of God that is within man and that is the vary realm of his divine being, immortal. A love creature created to respond to God in love in perfection and harmony. Man, as stated above, was born into the Divine life; he had the position of being in both heaven and earth. A spirit being, with a free will to choose, created to multiply and bring forth sons of like nature as that of God's perfection. Who also had contact with his Creator in heaven and on earth in perfect worship.

This was man in his original intended state.

"And the LORD God planted a garden eastward in Eden; and there he put the man whom he had formed." Genesis 2:8

"And out of the ground made the LORD God to grow every tree that is pleasant to the sight, and good for food; the tree of life also in the midst of the garden, and the tree of knowledge of good and evil."

Genesis 2:9

"the tree of life also in the midst of the garden, and the tree of knowledge of good and evil. But of the tree of the knowledge of good and evil, you shall not eat of it: for in the day that you eat thereof you shall surely die." Genesis 2:16-17

This is the first law given with blessing (eat freely of) and a curse (shall surely die). This death is separation from God spiritually and brings man to physical death, as it is part of this curse. It is to have eyes that can't see and ears that don't hear spiritual things. Because mans spirit is asleep, as a seed in a dormant state, covered by a hard shell, which causes man to live in darkness under the influence of Satan, as seen in Genesis 3:16-20. This is the first rebellion by disobedience of man.

Adam's first signs of craving or desiring through reasoning is for the knowledge of the nature of the animal and plant world. Something was influencing him to notice that things were different about the animals. They were two separate beings of male and female and Adam was one. Something is causing a stronger draw on him than his normal relationship with God and His love. This desire in Adam is what caused the tree of the knowledge of good and evil to grow, and produce its fruit. God warns man not to eat of it because He knows that when Adam does eat of that fruit, he will suffer death, in anguish and pain all the days of his life, in fear and strife. He has caused the death of his eternal nature (immortality) and love of God his creator, and has lost all dominion of all created things and become subject to them instead. He has then taken on the nature of sin and death, the result of which is corruption and disease of the earthy body and ends in his eternal death.

The animals are not ignorant of what concerns them, they have a sensible intuitive instinct and knowledge of everything that is required and how to go about getting it. They only focus on food, shelter, protection and reproduction. It is that Adam desired the knowledge of. Which all has resulted in the knowledge and desire of the natural world, of nature, or the spirit of the world (Satan's) deception, materialism, wealth, desire for things, and the bestial nature of sex, and more. Mankind has just gone spiraling out of control with this knowledge.

Genesis 2:18

"The LORD God said, "It is not good that the man should be alone; I will make him an help meet for him."

Adam's desire was for a mate to bring completion to him as he saw with the animals. He didn't realize he already was complete.

Genesis 2:21-25

"The LORD God caused a deep sleep* to fall upon Adam, and he slept: and He took one of his ribs, and closed up the flesh instead thereof; And the rib, which the LORD God had taken from man, made he a woman, and brought her to the man. Adam said, "This is now bone of my bones, and flesh of my flesh: she shall be called Woman, because she was taken out of Man. Therefore shall a man leave his father and his mother, and shall cleave unto his wife: and they shall be one flesh." They were both naked, the man and his wife, and were not ashamed."**

*   *Hebrew and Aramaic means: to exchange one thing for another, it also means to repeat the exchange a second time.*
**   *the glory of God covered them so they knew not their nakedness even before God.*

Genesis 3:1-3

"Now the serpent was more subtle (*crafty, cunning, prudent*) than any beast of the field which the LORD God had made. He (*the serpent*) said to the woman, "to you, has God said, You shall not eat of every tree of the garden?" The woman said to the serpent, "We may eat of the fruit of the trees of the garden: But of the fruit of the tree which is in the middle of the garden, God has said, we shall not eat of it, neither shall you touch it, lest we die."*

*   *Hebrew and Aramaic meaning: The pictograph m is a picture of water representing chaos, the t is a picture of two crossed sticks representing a mark or sign. Combined these mean "chaos mark". The length of time that something exists and ends, mute; moot—as a dead point; mortal—with*

an additional r and l; mate—of "check mate" meaning "king is dead".
Taken from the Ancient Hebrew Lexicon of the Bible

Genesis 3:4-6

"The serpent said to the woman, "you shall not surely die: For God does know that in the day you eat thereof, then your eyes shall be opened, and you shall be as gods, knowing good and evil." When the woman saw that the tree was good for food, and that it was pleasant to the eyes, and a tree to be desired to make one wise, she took of the fruit thereof, and did eat, and gave also to her husband with her; and he did eat."

The chief angel, Satan (the first deceived self, pride, covetousness), also called the dragon, that led the rebellion, who took with him, his regiment (1/3 of all angels), when thrown out of the presence of God and of Heaven, taking a portion of the angels. And corrupted the earth which underwent even more corruption and compaction because of the curse (Revelations chapter twelve). He is the spirit of the world that corrupts everything on it and in it. Leading many by his deceptive "religare" Latin for religion, and its many divisions, which all hinder God Will and plan for mankind. Questioning the vary word of God, causing doubt, reasoning and unbelief birthed lust in the mind of the woman. Now the seed of self will, the desire or lust for the things of the bestial nature, has been given root in man through the disobedience, first of the woman, which caused him to lose the divine nature and in turn caused him to take on Satan's nature. The eyes of the flesh will be opened and the eyes of the spirit or soul will be closed or veiled in man, all which brings on the emotional aspect and living by one's "feelings". Adams free will choice separates him from being a spiritual being, that God had made him to be, and changes him into the bestial nature of the serpent, Satan. He takes on the animal nature of life, temporary as it is in its life to death, now in corruption, and is now subject to the worldly spirit and all manner of evil, demonic and makes him a slave to that nature. Or to be more precise, he then became a son of Satan. Ghastly as this sounds, it is absolutely what Adam and all his descendants are.

Genesis 3:7-8

"The eyes of them both were opened, and they knew that they were naked; and they sewed fig leaves together, and made themselves aprons. They heard the voice of the LORD God walking in the garden in the cool of the day: and Adam and his wife hid themselves from the presence of the LORD God amongst the trees of the garden."

The changing from a spiritual being to an earthy being, a soul creature with eyes to see and ears to hear only the natural things, no longer a divine being, living in the Kingdom of God. They now have sin consciousness, under the influence of all that is evil.

Genesis 3:9-12

"The LORD God called to Adam, and said to him, 'Where are you?' He said, "I heard your voice in the garden, and I was afraid, because I was naked; and I hid myself."* He said, 'Who told you that you were naked? Have you eaten of the tree, whereof I commanded you that you should not eat?' The man said, "The woman whom you gave to be with me, she gave me of the tree, and I did eat."

* *Sin causes fear and shame of that which was natural with God in holiness and sanctification of righteousness.*

He knew that separation had taken place, by His calling out to Adam. Sin causes fear and shame of that which was natural with God in holiness and sanctification of righteousness.

Genesis 3:13

"The LORD God said to the woman, 'What is this that you have done?' And the woman said, "The serpent beguiled me, and I did eat."

This is a spiritual separation from the nature and character of God, a separation from Christ both inward and outward, as their covering. Thusly putting man on the level of the animal life; fleshly, carnal, earthy. In the exchange of the divine nature and character of Christ to that of the nature and character of Satan, man is now blind to the things of God and has become open to the anguish of sin under the curse of that sin. Now a bond-slave to Satan and a lover of darkness rather than light. Matthew 6:23, 27:45, Luke 1:79, 11:34-35, John1:5, 3:19

Genesis 3:14-15

"The LORD God said to the serpent, 'Because you have done this, you are cursed above all cattle, and above every beast of the field; upon your belly shall you go, and dust shall you eat all the days of your life: And I will put enmity between you and the woman, and between your seed and her seed; it shall bruise your head, and you shall bruise his heel.'"

This is the verse (15) that we've been waiting for because within it we have a vow, a covenant given which covers the whole earth and all of humanity from Adam to every person who has ever been born or ever will be born, which this seed of life is imparted.

The nature and character of God and the glory of God, then only becomes a seed that God planted within woman. This seed then is passed on through woman to all humanity from then on. Mans blood is defiled, for life is in the blood. This seed contains all the nature and likeness of God in Christ but requires the operation of God in the fire, Light and Love, the Holy Spirit and the death of the bestial nature, for this seed to come to life again. An action of man's free will of choice, that allows the light of God contained in the Word (John1:1-5) and the Spirit to give life to this seed which quickens our spirit and soul. As a seed of grain has to have the outward husk or shell broken (this is the evil that sealed up the good of God) and die before the ovule can bring forth new life. God in Christ in man again in regeneration by redemption. This seed, when properly fed on the Word of God, then can grow into a large tree that is drawing its nourishment from the root which is also Christ the Father of mankind.

If all we read is taken, in the literal since, we miss the whole of it, and remain in our sin. But if we hear the figurative we will hear and see the Truth. Especially when Jesus stated 'in the volume of the book it is written of Me' (see also: Hebrews 10:1-6, 7-9, 10; 2:14; John 1:10,14). Again as we've already stated; He is our Redeemer and our redemption herein written of. For this is what John the Baptist meant when through his disciples he asked, "Are you the one that we're to look for?" Matthew 11:3 and Luke 7:19

When Jesus took the twelve into the upper room His was the second Adam in fulfillment of this covenant of redemption because He is both the redemption and Redeemer. Just as He is the greater one of promise in all Covenants all Psalms and the prophets. Also as Saul of Tarsus saw Him, as the Law and its giver, on the Damascus road. So when He said that He was the bread broken, He was broken by Israel. His flesh, the meat of the Living Word, is a testament of Him, that He is just that. When He said that His blood was the wine and as the root of Jesse, He IS the fruit of the vine. In fact all that He did was in agreement with this Covenant because He had the power and virtue within Him to make such statements. No other man has ever had the right to claim such, for all are made (procreated) in the union of man and woman, made in sin.

Genesis 3:16

"To the woman he said, 'I will greatly multiply your sorrow and your conception; in sorrow you shall bring forth children; and your desire shall be to your husband, and he shall rule over you.'"

Genesis 3:17-20

"To Adam he said, 'Because you have hearkened to the voice of your wife, and have eaten of the tree, of which I commanded you, saying, 'You shall not eat of it': cursed is the ground for your sake; in sorrow shall you eat of it all the days of your life; Thorns also and thistles shall it bring forth to you; and you shall eat the herb of the field; In the sweat of your face shall you eat bread, till you return to the ground; for out of it were you taken; for dust you are, and unto dust shall you return.' Adam called his wife's name Eve; because she was the mother of all living."

The results of mans eating now having the inward knowledge (the two tenets of all faith) of good and evil, and the ability to see Gods hand in all of the creation or nature around him (through mans conscience as the seed) his spiritual eyes and ears are now closed or veiled, darkened and turned inward. All mankind is without excuse for all is revealed to him by nature itself (and within man is that desire for his original nature to be restored again, known as anguish of conscience). The second encounter with deception and again the choice is turned to self-will against that which was commanded him, the vary thing that caused Satan to fall in the first place . . . PRIDE. Now man is the slave to the bestial nature and all of its ugly components consisting of: darkness, fire, thickness, death, wrath, disease and all the offspring of them. Which are but a reflection of Satan's character and nature.

Genesis 3:21-24

"To Adam also and to his wife did the LORD God made coats of
skins, and clothed them. The LORD God said, 'Behold, the man
is become as one of us, to know good and evil: and now, lest he
put forth his hand, and take also of the tree of life, and eat, and
live for ever': Therefore the LORD God sent him forth from the
garden of Eden, to till the ground from whence he was taken. So
he drove out the man; and he placed at the east of the garden of
Eden Cherubim, and a flaming sword which turned every way, to
keep the way of the tree of life."

The spirit of evil that is at work here on earth. We see it in
merchandising, worldliness and its passions of self-will and
their evil offspring, through reasonings, religion, philosophy,
intellectualism, the wisdom of man, mans imagination, emotions,
opinions, feelings, our five senses, self sufficiency, ect . . .

The establishing of this covenant, the placement of the seed of
redemption to re-establish the Kingdom of God in the soul and
spirit of man, through the Light and Truth of Christ, has brought
about the way for the death of mans selfish will and slavery to all
evil in his fallen nature, and the birth of Christ within man. This
new birth of Christ has reversed the operation of the fall of man
in the garden.

Man now finds himself with the promise of a coming redeemer
and His redemption for all mankind that will destroy the evil
nature that is at work in and through fallen man. God is setting
up for the wrath to come in the enmity of these two natures, that

of God and Satan. Man can only serve one, be governed by one or the other, not both simultaneously.

The curse placed upon the ground as given to Adam has effected all created creatures. Nature and creation waits in anguish for the revealing of the sons of God. All of creation has this consuming fire contained in it which is wrath and darkness, because the presence of God is removed. Adam, in disobedience to God, put out the Life, Light and Love of God (Christ in Grace) in himself and put all mankind, with the earthly creatures, into subjection of the natural realm of earth with this fallen nature, temporary as it is.

Man, from the time of his fall, is the carrier of the seed in his soul that will be the destroyer of the power of darkness, mans eternal separation from the Life, Love and Light of God. The redeemer will bring the Truth, the Way and the Life back into man, by light His redemption action. Man also carries the spiritual torch awaiting the flame to re-ignite the fire of Eternal Life. This is the promise to man given by God of the ability through redemption of the seed, to a spirit being again by re-genesis (regeneration, in restoration) and the future salvation in which man is now in hope for. Which brings man into righteousness and then through sanctification. This is the process of man's cleansing and restoring Gods character and nature in again. The perfection of what was and is now progressively being again.

God takes the first action of atonement, or propitiation, with the shedding of blood and the covering with the skins of an animal to cover their nakedness and the nature of sin and death. This is the first action of the covenant toward the recovery and redemption of man to a place of "at-one-ment" with his creator. No one ascends to heaven unless they are born again, born from above, through the re-genesis or regeneration into the eternal nature, the first true state of created man. This covenant was taught to the sons of Adam. Seth carries on in place of Abel who Cain, the earthy man, killed after reasoning within himself. Reasoning being his religion, "religare" and our first glimpse of it. Let's remember the "law of the first" hidden in scripture; the first born son is usually the spiritual one of the family when he is conceived according to God's program.

This however, is not the way God deals with the individual. He must deal first with the earthy nature, when the earthy is dealt with, then He can deal with the spiritual nature.

"Law of the first" is seen here in that He, Yehovah had created man, a complete being in himself and therefore take from that which was created to create again or pro-create, a mystery hidden in scripture because it was spoken and is the Word of God. A thing that angels can not do, they are not able to reproduce or pro-create in themselves. God is the self existent one. Man is a receptive creation, he depends upon an outside source for his existence, he can pro-create but he cannot produce anything on his own. It is the spirit that man chooses to reside under that is reflected in his character and nature.

Genesis 5:3

"When Adam had lived 130 years, he fathered a son in his own likeness, after his image, and named him Seth."

Seth carries on in place of Abel who Cain the earthy man killed. Seth is the father of Noah, Noah is the father of Shem, Shem is the great grand father of Eber a relative of Abram, [who will become known as Abraham] as found in the book of Jasher in it, it is told that Abram who at the age of ten stayed with Noah and Shem to learn the ways of the Lord for twenty-nine years. Shem, I believe, is the king of Salem and the high priest of the Most High God, otherwise known as Melchizedek.* His heirs, through Abraham, will become the children of Israel who will become the nation of promise through whom Yehovah will come in the flesh, as Immanuel, the Son of man, Jesus of Nazareth, the Messiah of Israel, the incarnation of Adam as the second Adam, mans promised Redeemer. Paul, by revelation, will show us that Christ is the Redeemer of the world and all mankind through whom will come Salvation to those who are willing to allow the reversal of death, and come into the Glorious Light of the New Covenant of Grace.

*   *This was given to me as a revelation some time ago. I don't say this frequently as some people see it.*

We have a good start in understanding the mysteries of God and the foundation upon which all covenants are based, including the ones given to Abraham, Isaac, Jacob, King David and any others. We will now take a look at a few of these covenants. We must listen very carefully and closely with special attention to the wording and phrases used by God in them to describe what He promises. The mysteries or secrets spoken of in Deuteronomy 29:29 are hidden within each of the Covenants or promises.

This had led many to a misunderstanding or misinterpretation in which they then lead others astray.

Genesis 12:1-5

"The LORD had said to Abram, Get out of thy country, and from thy kindred, and from thy father's house, to a land that I will show thee: And I will make of thee a great nation, and I will bless thee, and make thy name great; and thou shalt be a blessing: **And I will bless them that bless thee**, and curse him that curses thee*: and **in thee shall all families of the earth be blessed**. So Abram departed, as the LORD had spoken to him; and Lot went with him: and Abram was seventy and five years old when he departed out of Haran. And Abram took Sarai his wife, and Lot his brother's son, and all their substance that they had gathered, and the souls that they had gotten in Haran; and they went forth to go into the land of Canaan; and into the land of Canaan they came." (emphasis mine)

*   *If you are walking in the faith of Abraham you are blessed with his blessing but if you are **not** walking in the faith that Abraham walked, you are cursed with this curse. See 2 Corinthians 6:14-7:1*

Genesis 17:1-11

"When Abram was ninety years old and nine, the LORD appeared to Abram, and said to him, 'I am the Almighty God; **walk before me, and be thou perfect.** And I will make my covenant between me and thee, and will multiply thee exceedingly'. And Abram fell on his face: and God talked with him, saying, 'As for me, behold, my covenant *is* with thee, and thou shalt be a father of **many nations**. Neither shall thy name any more be called Abram, but thy name shall be Abraham; for **a father of many nations** have I made thee. And I will make thee exceeding fruitful, and I will make **nations** of thee, and kings shall come out of thee. And I will establish my covenant between me and thee and thy seed after thee in their generations for an everlasting covenant, to be a God unto thee, and to thy seed after thee. And I will give unto thee, and to thy seed after thee, the land wherein thou art a stranger, all the land of Canaan, for an everlasting possession; and I will be their God'. And God said unto Abraham, 'Thou shalt keep my covenant therefore, thou, and thy seed after thee in their generations. This is my covenant, which ye shall keep, between me and you and thy seed after thee; Every man child among you shall be circumcised. And ye shall circumcise the flesh of your foreskin; and it shall be a token of the covenant betwixt me and you'." (emphasis mine)

This is speaking of the "NEW" thing that God is bringing about through Christ. With our physical eyes and ears we see and hear God making a covenant to Abraham and his seed or descendents through Israel (Jacob) for the physical land of Canaan, to be carried out to those by the circumcision of the physical flesh, but . . . . and here is the BIG BUT . . . . God is making this covenant, "the everlasting covenant" with Abraham and his seed or descendants through FAITH, with Canaan actually being Christ, to be carried out to those by the circumcision of the spiritual heart. This is the ONLY way it is everlasting!! We all know that when two people or groups make a covenant it is good only as long as one or the other does not break it, or by the death of one or the other. We all also know, just by reading our Bible that Israel BROKE COVENANT many times over. We will not get into this now but will cover it later on.

Genesis 18:17-19

"The LORD said, '**Shall I hide from Abraham that thing which I do**; Seeing that Abraham shall surely become a great and mighty nation, and **all the nations of the earth** shall be blessed **in him**?* For I know him, that **he will command his children and his household** after him, and they **shall keep the way of the LORD**, to do justice and judgment; **that the LORD may bring upon Abraham that which he hath spoken of him'**." (emphasis mine)

*   *through or by walking in Abraham's faith, trusting as he trusted.*

Gen 22:15-18

"The angel of the LORD called unto Abraham out of heaven the second time, And said, 'By myself have I sworn', saith the LORD, 'for because thou hast done this thing, and hast not withheld thy son, thine only son; That in blessing I will bless thee, and in multiplying **I will multiply thy seed as the stars of the heaven**, and as the sand which is upon the sea shore; and thy seed shall possess the gate of his enemies; And **in thy seed shall all the nations of the earth be blessed**; because 'thou hast obeyed my voice'." (emphasis mine) See also; Matthew 10:37 and Luke 13:6-9

Notice the difference in the two groups, the stars of heaven and the sand of the sea? One is spiritual children, stars of heaven and the other is earthy children, sand of the sea. The spiritual are those who have given up the cravings and desires of all things earthy or natural and come out of all religion otherwise known as Babylon. They walk by faith, in the spirit and not by flesh or sight. They do not practice the rites, rituals and traditions of religion which is idolatry. Paul calls these people the **Israel of God** in Galatians 6:16.

Genesis 26:1b-4

"Isaac went unto Abimelech king of the Philistines unto Gerar. And the LORD appeared unto him, and said, 'Go not down into Egypt; dwell in the land which I shall tell thee of: Sojourn in this land, and I will be with thee, and will bless thee; for unto thee, and unto thy seed, I will give all these countries, and I will perform the oath which I swore unto Abraham thy father; And **I will make thy seed to multiply as the stars of heaven** and will give unto thy seed all these countries; and **IN thy seed shall all the nations of the earth be blessed**; Because that Abraham obeyed my voice, and kept my charge, my commandments, my statutes, and my laws'." (emphasis mine)

Genesis 28:12-16

"Jacob dreamed, and behold a ladder set up on the earth, and the top of it reached to heaven: and behold the angels of God ascending and descending on it. And, behold, the LORD stood above it, and said, 'I *am* the LORD God of Abraham thy father, and the God of Isaac:* the land whereon thou lies, to thee will I give it, and to thy seed; **And thy seed shall be as the dust of the earth**, and thou shalt spread abroad to the west, and to the east, and to the north, and to the south: and **in thee and in thy seed shall all the families of the earth be blessed**.** And, behold, I am with thee, and will keep thee in all places whither thou goest, and **will bring thee again into this land**; for I will not leave thee, **until I have done that which I have spoken to thee of***. And Jacob awoke out of his sleep, and he said, Surely the LORD is in this place; and I knew it not." (emphasis mine)

*   *He is their God, the God of the Living, because they walk IN faith, obeying all things He told them.*
** *IN the seed of faith which is Christ, shall all the nations be blessed.*
*** *God's plan and purpose is to bring us back into that place Adam was in before the fall. More on all this to come.*

Psalm 72:17

"His name shall endure for ever: his name shall be continued as long as the sun: and *men* shall be blessed in him: all nations shall call him blessed."

In each of the above listed passages are phrases such as, "in your seed shall all nations be blessed", "in you shall all the families of the earth be blessed", "I will make your seed to multiply as the stars of heaven", "a father of many nations" and the like. Each of these references are building blocks on the first promise spoken to Adam through whom will come the Redeemer of the world, as the seed of woman. The seed hidden within all mankind's soul, has given them all the ability to be saved and restored. To

Abraham, He said that those who would believe as he believes, a blessing will come and they will receive circumcision of the heart illustrated by the circumcision of the foreskin. Through our study we will trace these promises and covenants to find their intended outcome, in Christ.

ARE YOU SO BLIND THAT YOU CANNOT SEE?

These words ring constantly in my thoughts, the words of my Lord, "eyes to see and ears to hear and a heart to understand". We see many instances when Jesus walked this earth during His ministry to Israel, that He opened blind eyes and restored sight, and opened deaf ears to restore hearing. We see many times when He brought the dead back to life. These things He did, not for us to copy Him in, but rather to teach a spiritual lesson using a physical manifestation.

In one of our morning devotional studies I saw something I'd never seen before, although I had read this verse hundreds of times, and heard it preached many times. This verse is a favorite in today's missions. It's Matthew 28:20 Let's look at this a bit, but instead of looking at just that one verse, let's see what the whole thought is.

Jesus had been crucified and buried, and on the third day Mary Magdalene and the other Mary, had gone to the tomb. When they arrived, there was a great earthquake and the tomb was opened. The angel that greeted them asked them who they were looking for. They told him they were looking for Jesus the one who had been crucified. The angel then told them that He was no longer there, that He had risen. Just outside the tomb in the garden the women encountered a man whom they believed to be the gardener. To their great astonishment it was Christ the risen Lord! He told them to tell Peter and the others to meet Him in Galilee, and so they did. Here we begin;

Matthew 28:16-20

"Then the eleven disciples went away into Galilee, into a mountain where Jesus had appointed them. And when they saw Him, they worshiped Him: but some doubted.

And Jesus came and spake unto them, saying, "All power is given unto Me in heaven and in earth.

Go ye therefore, and teach all nations, baptizing them in the name of the Father, and of the Son, and of the Holy Ghost: Teaching them to observe all things whatsoever I have commanded you: and, lo, I am with you always, even unto the end of the world."

There are a few things I want to point out here. First of all, to clarify things, Jesus the risen Lord, is speaking only to His eleven disciples, remember Judas is dead. Here we have what is referred to as "The Great Commission" Go ye therefore, teach all nations, baptizing them in the name . . . ." Now here we have some words that we don't think about much. We act presumptuously, thinking we know what this is saying and who it's being said to. But, we don't! We knowingly or unknowingly disregard it.

Then we disobey it.

These words are:

NATIONS; what nations? Only the ones that the Jews scattered to. Remember they had been told to stay away from the Gentiles. Not to go into a Gentiles home or have anything to do with them, at least not at this time. Jesus stated in Matthew 10:6 and Matthew 15:24 that He had come ONLY to the lost sheep of the house of Israel. Their going to the Gentiles didn't happen until Paul came on the scene.

BAPTIZE IN THE NAME; pay close attention to this here. The Jews baptized in water for repentance.

The "baptizer" would baptize the "baptizee" saying to them, "In the name of the Father, Son and Holy Ghost, I baptize thee" or something like that. So, what he was actually doing was immersing him into the name. Jesus had said to them earlier that "whatsoever you shall ask IN my Name, it shall be done." Now all they needed at that time was to be IN His name. And they were, that's why they were able to perform so many miracles. Let's continue . . . .

The word OBSERVE; Jesus taught them to observe the laws and commandments as they traveled around. The things He told them to observe here are simply their Jewish laws and ordinances. They were to stay in the "state" they were in, or to remain in their Jewishness. He, Jesus, never told them (while on the earth) to come out of the the house of Israel, but when that age ended things changed.

The part that struck me the most was when He told them, *"lo, I am with you always, even unto the end of the world."* Did you hear that? Did you REALLY HEAR WHAT HE JUST SAID? Jesus, our Risen Lord had just told the disciples that He would be WITH them . . . . until when? UNTIL THE END OF THE WORLD!

We all know that eternity is never ending. So, why did Christ say what He said here to the disciples? Let's examine these words then. I'm using the Strong's Hebrew/Greek Dictionary and the Thayer's Greek Dictionary.

WITH: A primary preposition (often used adverbially); properly denoting *accompaniment*; "amid" with which it is joined; with, after, behind

UNTO: Of uncertain affinity; a conjugation, preposition and adverb of continuance, *until* (of time and place):—even (until, unto), (as) far (as), how long, to, while, till, until

END: *entire completion*, that is, *consummation* (of a dispensation): —end. completion, consummation, end

WORLD (OR AGE): properly an *age*; by extension *perpetuity* (also past); by implication the *world*; specifically (Jewish) a Messianic period (present or future):—age, course, eternal,

Please note that the translators here in the Strong's has the word "eternal", but again we know that if it's ETERNAL it is NEVER ENDING!

ETERNAL: *perpetual* (also used of past time, or past and future as well):—eternal, for ever, everlasting, world (began).

Here's the **Thayer Definition:**

1) without beginning and end, that which always has been and always will be
2) without beginning
3) without end, never to cease, everlasting

So now, why would Jesus tell the disciples that He will be WITH them UNTIL the END of the WORLD?

Let's go now and look at the prayer that Jesus prayed before His death, burial and resurrection, in John 17. I'm not putting the whole prayer in here, please go read it for yourself. But, I will put a couple of key verses and phrases in so you get the picture of what's going on.

John 17:2 As thou hast given Him (Jesus) power over all flesh, that he should give **eternal life** to as many as thou hast given him.

John 17:3 And this is **life eternal**, that they might know thee the only true God, and Jesus Christ, whom thou hast sent.

John 17:17 Sanctify them through thy truth: **thy word is truth.**

John 17:19 And for their sakes I sanctify myself*, that **they also** might be **sanctified through the truth.**

John 17:21 That they all may be one; as thou, Father, *art* in me, and I in thee, that they also may be one in us:

John 17:23 I in them, and thou in me, that they **may be made perfect in one;**

Here we see Jesus praying for the ones the Father had given Him. In this prayer you will see that He did NOT pray for the world. Only those given Him through the call before the last Passover and His death on the cross. He does pray for them to become one in Him and He is one with Father.

* This is interesting in that even Jesus was sanctified. How? Remember this was just before He went to the cross, and on that cross He put to death all deeds of the flesh . . . this is what we must do to be sanctified as well. However, we must be put to death by faith in Him.

We must not be so blinded by our own opinions or religious traditions that we cannot see that Israel, The Jews, were to be the ones leading the rest of the world into this faith. They were blind to the fact, that although they were a special people, chosen by God for a specific work, that they were not the only ones God called. They kept themselves separate from all others, to the point of self appointed exclusivity of their nationalism, but still managed to disobey God and get into the idolatries of the nations around them. That very exclusivity became an idol itself. Although they were given many warnings from God through the prophets, they wouldn't heed them at all and even killed the prophets so as not to hear them. They continued on and on in this fraudulent manner until the time appointed that God destroyed Judaism. He then turned to the Gentiles and the

Jews went berserk. Paul, before when he was Saul of Tarsus, was even in one killing the ones that entered into faith, until that day when the LORD literally knocked him on his backside! Paul continued preaching to the Jews but they would hear none of it so he brushed the dust from his hands and feet and went to the Gentiles. Around 70 AD, God had the Temple destroyed, but the Jews, even up to this day, continue in that idolatry by trying to keep the Judaistic exclusivity alive.

Allow the scales to fall from your eyes and come out from the blindness of Israel, just as it happened to Paul as recorded in Acts 9.

ISRAEL'S BLINDNESS WHICH LEADS TO BLINDNESS OF THE CHURCH

I n this chapter we will show the blindness of Israel and their rejection of Christ. We will work our way on through to the blindness of the Gentile nations as they run parallel to Israel in this rejection.

Romans is a letter which starts the revealing of Christ's finished work of the cross and how God sees humanity. The mystery of Israel's blindness is found at the end of the parenthetical clause found at the beginning of Romans 9 through 11. All this is dealing with Israel's past, presents and future, with chapter 12 picking up again the teaching from the end of chapter 8.

Paul, in the first five chapters of his letter to the Romans, beginning at chapter 1 verses 18 through to 32, reveals how God sees the immoral man. In chapter 2 verses 1 through 16; God reveals how He sees the moral man, then in verse 17 through chapter 3 verse 20; God reveals how He sees the religious man. God reveals, through Paul, in chapter 3 verses 19 to 27 the removal of doubt, and telling us to NOT doubt as Israel did. Again in chapter 3 verse 19 through chapter 4 verse 8, we find the promise of Redemption and justification in righteousness. Beginning at chapter 4 through chapter 5 verse 5, we have imputed "right-wise-ness" the result of justification through the finished work of the cross. Paul overlaps this action of God from chapter 3 verse 26 on through chapter 4 verse 9, to strengthen the foundation as contained in the finished work of the cross of Christ; and our being in Christ in God's mystical power of grace, the "It is finished" of Jesus' flesh being put to death and mans sin problem done with forever. The secret of our being identified (conjoined) in Christ in His selfless action of love by allowing man to put Him to death on that tree and taking on the wrath and punishment due us. All this was done because of the action of Adam when he put to death the Christ of God that he contained in himself as a divine being.

Christ, as the second Adam, brings redemption in His blood unto regeneration of mans spirit to newness of life to be quickened from the dead, that condition natural man still lives in. In this condition man lives according to his flesh or natural senses/sensuality. The ones truly born to this new life still contains the flesh or the outward man but the new spiritual man is to learn to keep it in subjection. This is done by the power of the Holy Spirit in Faith by putting the desires or lusts of the flesh to death daily, as they raise their ugly head. We may even think of this as regaining the dominion over the earth that God gave to Adam in the beginning. As we hold this dominion over our own bodies and minds, God sees that we are approved to hold it over other things on the earth. This is known as crucifying the flesh or taking up the cross of Christ daily.

Then in chapter 4 verse 1 through chapter 5 verse 5, Paul reveals our righteousness in Christ in God when we, by faith, acquire or accept the truth of God's working for us and in us for His good pleasure, our total redemption by sanctification. This requires our being literally removed from that death and sin nature and conjoined again with Christ as Adam was in the garden. Adam was given a commandment not to eat of a certain tree in the garden, but he did anyway and caused the death of his union with Christ in God. This death of that union is the condition that mankind is in still today. As innocent as newborn babies are, they are in this condition and exercise that state of rebellion as they grow physically. Jesus came to restore us back into that union or conjoining with Himself and God and this could only be done through His death on that cross. He died the very death that Adam died, but in reverse.

It is something that no man, in any works done by the flesh, could or would accomplish. For if we could we would have something to boast about before God and this we cannot do, because God has done it all for us when we, by His Faith, receive it. This was a sovereign working of God and was His plan, held in secret from before the foundation of the world. A mystery now revealed to those who are in Christ Jesus, as Paul was chief, or first of this line or group under the Headship of Christ. There are hints of this plan in the Old Testament through the Psalms and prophets. They searched for the meaning of the secrets but were unable to find the key to unlock the meaning of those hints. Ezekiel was told to eat the roll, then go speak His Words to the house of Israel (Ezekiel 3:1-6). Daniel was told in chapter 12 verse 4, to close the words and seal up the book even unto the end; many will run to and fro and increase in knowledge. This is something we see quite a lot of now. Men attempting to gather as much knowledge as they can through books and teachings of other men. However, they are not finding these mysteries revealed because to them they are sealed up. Only the Holy Spirit can divulge the secrets of God to you. Otherwise all they are then, are the blind leading the blind and false prophets and teachers. They have not been found approved by God as worthy stewards of the mysteries of God.

Still in Romans, in chapter 5 verse 6, we find the struggle with the law of sin and death, and it's power that Paul had in his flesh, that we all struggle with as well. This is the crucifying of the old Adam nature in our flesh as spoken of earlier, through to the end of chapter 5. In chapters 6 through 8, Paul again shows us what he had covered earlier, in order to strengthen our faith and the workings which God accomplished through Christ. We see this in Paul's illustration of the battle of the two natures. The wisdom of God contained in Christ, is then revealed in and through those who possess the Ontological Essence of the Spirit of Christ as well as the Spirit of God (Romans 8:9). Continuing in chapter 8, we see in verses 14 through 17 what many call "the Romans road to salvation." However the plan of our salvation can better be seen in 1 Corinthians 15: 1-8. This is referred to as a "road" in the sense of an ongoing event. It is not something that is static or one time only. It is a continual operation of growth until the time the body of flesh is changed into His Glory and we see Him face to face, as He is . . . so are we.

Chapters 9, 10, and 11 are dealing with Israel's past, present, and future. Chapter 11 verse 25 is revealing Israel's blindness or hardness of heart.* From the first verse foreword Paul is explaining the error of Israel and why God laid aside the promised glory that Israel was to some day have. The purpose is for the benefit of the Gentiles and their entry into God's Gospel of Grace, because of Israel's doubting God, which is unbelief, and their failure to accept Jesus as their nation's promised Messiah and King.

Chapter 12 picks up where Paul left off at the end of chapter 8 with more of his teaching on the grace of God which is now available to all, both Jew and Gentile on a level playing field.

Chapter 16 is an addition to the letter written to the Romans in commendation to Phoebe, a sister in the Lord, in love for the love that she has shown in ministering to the Lord's servants, which ends in verse 24 with what we would call a "P.S.". Here, Paul adds another mystery, the fact that the gospel of grace revealed here a hidden secret of Christ's resurrection, as it was written in the scriptures and prophets, and is now made manifest to all the nations in faith, to obedience of faith. This gospel has power to establish all by the preaching of Christ. This mystery, which is the revealing of Israel's blindness, or hardness of heart, which started when Moses brought them out of Egypt, and has carried all the way up to this vary day.

* *Remember that Israel as a nation was lead by Priests that the Lord called false teachers, wolves, liars and whited sepulcher which appears beautiful outwardly but inwardly are full of dead mans bones and all uncleanness. These men taught lies and sowed doubt which is unbelief by reasoning's, which are the works of the devil. That is why Paul's letter to the Hebrews is a letter of persuasion to come out of a works gospel and a works mentality into a faith in God, a changing of the Hebrews thinking pattern and to a love of your neighbor working which is an obedience of faith in both love and grace.*

God does not want the Body of Christ ignorant of His plan as Israel was at the Lords first advent. He wants us to know the secrets and have complete knowledge of them, being able to teach others and to edify the Body of Christ with the reality of the truth. Each member of the Body is to strengthen each other to stand against all the wiles of the adversary as he attempts to draw us away from our faith in Christ's finished works and our being IN Him as one. He, the adversary, all the while is trying to keep us bound up in that religion, but for us to have our hope held steadfast in glory and our promise of eternal life with God in Christ, we must forever break those bonds of religion, and the only way this can be done is to "come out from among them" as Abraham was instructed to do by God when he left his homeland, and Paul told the Corinthians in 2 Corinthians 6:12-7:1. The Body is to be free from all bondage, that includes religion, nationalism, ethnicity, . . . ect. We have no identity other than Christ when we are One Body in Christ. We have chosen to give up or "die" to all other identification. Oh, we remain the same color of skin, and the place of our birth remains the same, but if we are truly ONE IN Christ, we are equal. If we say we are Christian, then continue to segregate ourselves from others, as in denominations or religions, we are actually denying Christ and fooling ourselves.

Paul, in the verses before this, is showing by the use of illustration, the olive tree. Christ is the trunk or vine of this tree with branches grafted in from a wild olive tree, this indicating the Gentiles. In chapters 7 and 8 he deals with the law and the fact that Israel was under the Law of Moses that God had given him. It made no room for forgiveness or charity. The Gentiles were under the first commandment given to man in Adam and that all humanity is required to die to this law of sin and death, this law of commandment was first spoken to man in Genesis 2:16-17, they were all Gentiles at that time, and were not, nor had they any part of Israel's Law. In another place he tells us that Jesus took the requirements of both laws to the cross and nailed them there in the sin filled flesh of man. Jesus tells us in the synoptic gospels, that He was the gate and the door through which it is required to enter the new birth by death to the sin nature. As Jesus acted in His own free will in obedience to death, we are by our own free will required to yield our hellish wills to the Father and see ourselves on the cross of Christ in death to the evil bondage of the flesh and man's religious traditions. Thereby willing to do His Will, and breaking the chains of bondage of sin and death, slaves to Satan's rule held in the flesh of natural man.

Israel blatantly rejected the kingdom of God, that had been promised to them, by the stoning of Stephen in Acts chapters 6 and 7 and when Stephen said that he saw the heavens opened and the Son of Man standing by the right hand of the throne of God (verse 56). Stephen used the phrase "Son of Man" same as Jesus used to describe Himself during His ministry on earth, which was to the nation of Israel primarily. This was the same phrase used by the prophet Ezekiel to describe the coming Messiah. As we look at Israel's partial hardening or blindness caused by its sin of unbelief, we can see this blindness is to cause Israel to become jealous of the Gentiles because of God's love being shown them and their acceptance as heirs and joint heirs of Christ in the kingdom of God through grace. This jealousy was to cause Israel to repent and turn to the Messiah, their Redeemer, and enter into the grace of God in Christ. They were to give up all the traditions, rites and rituals which had become idols and still are to this day.

Romans 11:25-32

"Lest you be wise in your own sight, **I want you to understand this mystery; a partial hardening has come upon Israel, until the fullness of the Gentiles has come in. In this way all Israel will be saved,** as it is written, 'The Deliverer will come from Zion, and he will banish ungodliness from Jacob; and this will be my covenant with them when I take away their sins.' As regards **the gospel, they are enemies of God for your sake.** But **as regards election, they are beloved for the sake of their forefathers.** For the gifts and the calling of God are irrevocable. For just as you were at one time disobedient to God but now have received mercy (*the gift of* **God**) because of their disobedience (*unbelief*), so **they too have now been disobedient**(*in unbelief*) **in order that by the mercy shown to you they also may now receive mercy.** For God has consigned all to disobedience, that he may have mercy on all."

Before we continue let me show you another version of this same passage of scripture taken from the Weymouth 1912 New Testament for comparison:

Romans 11:25-32

"For there is a truth, brethren, not revealed hitherto, of which I do not wish to leave you in ignorance, for fear you should attribute superior wisdom to yourselves—the truth, I mean, that partial blindness has fallen upon Israel until the great mass of the Gentiles have come in; and so all Israel will be saved. As is declared in Scripture, "FROM MOUNT ZION A DELIVERER WILL COME: HE WILL REMOVE ALL UNGODLINESS FROM JACOB; AND THIS SHALL BE MY COVENANT WITH THEM; WHEN I HAVE TAKEN AWAY THEIR SINS." In relation to the Good News, the Jews are God's enemies for your sakes; but in relation to God's choice they are dearly loved for the sake of their forefathers. For God does not repent of His free gifts nor of His call; but just as you were formerly disobedient to Him, but now have received mercy at a time when they are disobedient, so now they also have been disobedient at a time when you are receiving mercy; so that to them too there may now be mercy. For God has locked up all in the prison of unbelief, that upon all alike He may have mercy."

I showed you this other version so you could get a handle on what is being said here. God has called all of mankind and offered the free gift of grace through Christ. These are the gifts and callings that He will never revoke. However, we ourselves can cause them to not come about through our stubborn rebellion and refusal to accept them. When we get so "hung up" in our traditions, and think that we are the ones bringing about our own salvation by following these rites, rituals and traditions, which are nothing more than doctrines of demons disguised as man. This is when we become "wise in our own sight" we see ourselves higher and better than we actually are. To see ourselves as God sees us would be a horrendous shock! We are nothing at all, but still He loves us and wants us as His children.

In the introduction, I talked about "inattentional blindness". This was the cause of Israel's blindness, in that they would not receive Christ because their brains had only been prepared to comprehend that which was so deeply ingrained in them through the centuries. Take a quick look at Mary when she conceived Jesus in her womb. Out of all the maidens in Israel that had been told the prophesies of this conception, she was the only one truly prepared to comprehend and therefore to receive. When we are so engrossed in our own ways we will not receive Christ either. We may come to the alter of salvation but what are we receiving at that time? We repeat the sinners prayer and get all emotional and believe we have received the fullness of God. Sorry to disappoint you but that is not so. At that time, you have only received THE POWER TO BECOME a child of God. Your refusal to die to your own ways and traditions (including all denominations) and come out from among them, causes your abortion.

The partial blindness or hardening of Israel, spoken of in Romans 11:25 as a mystery, was because they actually wanted the Messiah, but when He showed up they couldn't comprehend Him as such. They were conditioned to expect, not the spiritual freedom Christ came to give, but rather a militaristic freedom from the oppression of the Roman Empire. They only comprehended the physical not spiritual. Even to this day, Israel and many in the Christian community, think that the nation of Israel is the apple of God's Eye. Not so, but it's the spiritual descendents of Abraham's seed which is Christ that are the "Israel of God" and the apple of His eye. They will continue to think this until such time as the fullness of the Gentiles has come in along with any individual Hebrew who has chosen Christ and His freedom over his Judaism, and has come out. Until such time as the Hebrews come out of their Jewish nationalism and Christians (as they call themselves) come out of their wrongful beliefs of the same, they are all enemies of God and the footstool of Christ.

Romans 11:1-2

"I ask, then, has God rejected his people? By no means! For I myself am an Israelite, a descendant of Abraham, a member of the tribe of Benjamin. God has not rejected his people whom he foreknew. Do you not know what the Scripture says of Elijah, how he appeals to God against Israel?"

Now a point needs to be made here as Paul uses the terms of argument heard in the Temple among the priests. They would start by saying something like: "I'm of the tribe of Levi or Benjamin"; just as Paul here is doing. However, Paul is NOT continuing to call himself a Jew.

Romans 11:7-14

"What then? Israel failed to obtain what it was seeking. The elect obtained it, but the rest were hardened, as it is written, "God gave them a spirit of stupor, eyes that would not see and ears that would not hear, down to this very day." David says, 'Let their table become a snare and a trap, a stumbling block and a retribution for them; let their eyes be darkened so that they cannot see, and bend their backs forever. I ask, did they stumble in order that they might fall? By no means! Rather through their trespass redemption has come to the Gentiles, so as to make Israel jealous. Now if their trespass means riches for the world, and if their failure means riches for the Gentiles, how much more will their full inclusion mean!" Now I am speaking to you Gentiles. Inasmuch then as I am an apostle to the Gentiles, I magnify my ministry in order somehow to make my fellow Jews jealous, and thus save some of them."

Notice in the last sentence Paul speaks of his "fellow Jews"? He says that because he HAD BEEN one. But now, he is no longer. He is one with Christ and therefore neither Jew nor Greek. Once you have become one in Christ you will lose the recognition and reputation that you once had. You will become a new creature in Christ. Paul was known as the one who persecuted those of "The Way" but that reputation soon fell away from him and he was known differently.

Romans 11:15

"For if their rejection means the reconciliation of the world, what will their acceptance mean but life from the dead?"

Life from the dead is in reference to life now in this present earthy state not only for Israel but all of mankind. For this is what was promised Adam in Genesis 3:15 and which the covenant of chapter 12:3 spoken to Abraham says "and the nations shall be blessed through you" "in thee shall all families of the earth be blessed." This is repeated in 18:18, 22:18, 26:4

We think of ourselves as living, but according to the Bible we are not. Because we in our natural state, since the fall of Adam, are dead to God and His influences. We are, contrary to common belief, under the rule of the prince of the power of the air or put another way, under the influence of the spirit of the world Satan, as slaves to his whims and by this we are enmity or hostility to God. Until we willfully become obedient to the requirements of God and put to death that spirit of sin and in death which are the lusts of the flesh. To no longer obey its voice, and it has no sway or influence over us. We become conjoined with Christ in His death and seated within Him at the right hand of God. We receive the kingdom of the Father of spirits restored within us just as Christ Jesus taught.

Romans 11:16-24

"And if the first fruit (of dough) is holy, so is the lump: and if the root is holy, so are the branches. But if some of the branches were broken off, and you, being a wild olive, were grafted in among them, and did become partaker with them of the root of the fatness of the olive tree; glory not over the branches: but if you glory, it is not you that bear the root, but the root you. You will say then, 'Branches were broken off, and that I might be grafted in.' Well; by their unbelief they were broken off, and you stand by your faith. Be not high-minded, but fear: for if God spared not the natural branches, neither will He spare you. Behold then the goodness and severity of God: toward them that fell, severity; but toward you, God's goodness, if you continue in His goodness: otherwise you also shall be cut off. And they also, if they continue not in their unbelief, shall be grafted in: for

God is able to graft them in again. For if you were cut out of that which is by nature a wild olive tree, and were grafted contrary to nature into a good olive tree; how much more shall these, which are the natural branches, be grafted into their own olive tree?"

This is where many come to think of the Nation of Israel as being a special people still. Yes, they were created and groomed to be a special priesthood to minister and direct all the nations to come into the kingdom of God. However, they didn't do this, did they? They lost the vision of what they were to be and do and became a nation of idolaters in the idolization of themselves and their position or religion. The Messiah was coming to them first to bring them into the spiritual realm or kingdom of heaven or God, so they could be the priests to the nations, but they refused because they did not comprehend. They saw or heard only that which their brains would allow.

Romans 15:3-10

"For Christ did not please himself, but as it is written, "The reproaches of those who reproached you fell on me." For whatever was written in former days was written for our instruction (*in learning*), that through endurance and through the encouragement of the Scriptures we might have hope. May the God of endurance and encouragement grant you to live in such harmony with one another, in accord with Christ Jesus that together you may with one voice glorify the God and Father of our Lord Jesus Christ. Therefore welcome one another as Christ has welcomed you, for the glory of God. For I tell you that Christ became a servant to the circumcised to show God's truthfulness, in order to confirm the promises given to the patriarchs, and in order that the Gentiles might glorify God for His mercy. As it is written, "Therefore I will praise you among the Gentiles, and sing to your name." And again it is said, "Rejoice, O Gentiles, with his people."

2Corinthians 3:4-18

"This is the confidence that we have through Christ toward God. Not that we are sufficient in ourselves to claim anything as coming from us, but our sufficiency is from God, who has made us competent to be ministers of a new covenant,(*a new and living way*) not of the letter but of the Spirit. For the letter kills, but the Spirit gives life. Now if the ministry of death, carved in letters on stone, came with such glory that the Israelites could not gaze at Moses' face because of its glory, which was being **brought to an end**, will not the ministry of the Spirit have even more glory? For if there was glory in the ministry of condemnation (*the Mosaic Law with its ordinances*), the ministry of righteousness must far exceed it in glory (*God's Grace*). Indeed, in this case, what once had glory has come to have no glory at all, because of the glory that surpasses it. (*The new life found only in Christ by Grace.*) For if what was being brought to an end came with glory, how much more will what is permanent have glory. Since we have such a hope, (*a more sure foundation, bed rock who is Christ)* we are very bold, not like Moses, who would put a veil over his face so that the Israelites might not gaze at the outcome of what was being brought to an end (*Jesus Christ was the end of the Mosaic Law with it's ordinances, for He fulfilled the requirements of it*). But their minds were hardened. For to this day, when they read the old covenant, that same veil remains unlifted, because only through (in) Christ is it taken away. Yes, to this day whenever Moses is read a veil lies over their hearts. But when one turns **into** the Lord, **the veil is removed**. Now the Lord is the Spirit, and where the Spirit of the Lord is, there is freedom. We all, with unveiled face, beholding the glory of the Lord, are being **transformed into the same image** from one degree of glory to another. This comes from the Lord who is the Spirit that abides forever." (emphasis mine)

Paul is telling us here, from Whom he learned or received this Truth. And Peter tells his followers to pay close attention to what Paul says and reveals as it carries a greater weight than Moses' writings, although some of the things Paul says is hard to understand. (2 Peter 3:10-18) We are to understand these mysteries and secrets! I've heard many people say that we cannot ever understand them while on earth, only when we get face to face with God will we then comprehend them. But I'm here to tell you that if you do not understand them NOW, you will never become face to face with Him in Glory! Jesus said many times and in many places that those who have eyes to see and ears to hear will know these secrets and be the ones to come into the kingdom! This is not just an option, but it's a requirement or mandate given by God, in order to become a son of God here and now!

2Corinthians 4:1-11

"Therefore, having this ministry by the mercy of God, we do not lose heart. But we have renounced disgraceful, underhanded ways. We refuse to practice cunning or to tamper with God's word, but by the open statement of the truth we would commend ourselves to everyone's conscience in the sight of God. Even if our gospel is veiled, ***it is veiled only to those who are perishing***. In their case the god of this world has blinded the minds of the unbelievers, to keep them from seeing the light of the gospel of the glory of Christ, who is the image of God. For what we proclaim is not ourselves, but **Jesus Christ as Lord**, with ourselves as your servants for Jesus' sake. For it is God, who said, "Let light shine out of darkness," has shone in our hearts to give the light of the knowledge of the glory of God in the face of Jesus Christ. We have this treasure in jars of clay, (*our flesh*) to show that the surpassing **power belongs to God and not to us**. We are afflicted in every way, but not crushed; perplexed, but not driven to despair; persecuted, but not forsaken; struck down, but not destroyed; always carrying in the body the death of Jesus, so that the life of Jesus may also be manifested in our bodies. For we who live are always being given over to death for Jesus' sake, so that the life of Jesus also may be manifested in our mortal flesh." (emphasis mine)

If we do not put to death our relationship with the spirit of the world or Satan, that is controlling this body, allowing it to speak and exalt itself over Christ, then the Life of Jesus cannot be manifested in our bodies. He's may be in our spirit and soul, but we need to give Him full reign of our bodies as well. We want healing in our bodies and well being, but we will never have that as long as the Life of Christ is not able to grow and penetrate through to the surface. Jesus told us that we cannot serve two masters. We will love one but hate the other. In other words we will allow one to be forceful and in control while quenching the other. Unfortunately, too many times the flesh wins out and we serve it and the spirit of the world instead of Christ, all the while calling ourselves Christians, and doing all the "churchy" things in and of ourselves, having quenched the Spirit of God and Christ. I can only imagine God and Christ shaking their heads and crying. This is why Jesus said that many will say, "Lord, Lord" but He will then tell then the He never knew them. They argue that they did all these things "in His name and for His glory" but He still says He never knew them and for them to depart as they are workers of iniquity. This is what got Paul so upset with the Corinthian Church. They were still greatly immature and not advancing as they should. Our own stubbornness and lack of comprehension will keep us from seeing and hearing that which The Spirit is saying and doing.

1Corinthians 2:4-16

"My speech and my preaching were not in persuasive words of wisdom, but in demonstration of the Spirit and of power:* that your faith should not stand in the wisdom of men, but in the power of God. We speak wisdom, however, among them that are full-grown: yet wisdom not of this world, nor of the rulers of this world, who are coming to naught: but we speak God's wisdom in a mystery, the wisdom that has been hidden, which God foreordained before the worlds *(were formed)* to our glory: which none of the rulers of this world had known: for had they known it, they would not have crucified the Lord of glory: but as it is written, Things which eye saw not, and ear heard not, and entered not into the heart of man, Whatsoever things God prepared for them that love Him. To us God revealed them through the Spirit: for the Spirit searches all things, yes, and the deep things of God. For who among men knows the things of a man, save (*except*) the spirit of the man, which is in him? (*Is the spirit of man alive or yet dead because of sin?*) Even so the things of God none knows save (*except*) the Spirit of God. We received, not the spirit of the world, again, but the spirit which is from God; that we might know the things that were freely given to us of (*by*) God. Which things also we speak, not in words which man's wisdom teaches, but which the Spirit teaches; combining spiritual things with spiritual words. Now the natural man receives not the things of the Spirit of God: for they are foolishness to him; and he cannot know them, because they are spiritually judged (*understood, discerned*). He that is spiritual judges (*understands and discerns*) all things, and he himself is judged of no man.** For who has known the mind of the Lord, that he should instruct him? But we have the mind of Christ."

Only when we have yielded our will to His Will in the required way, which is by death to the flesh of sins nature, do we respond to the word of the Lord spoken to us and heard by us in our spirit, we know it is truth.

*   *this is the resurrection power that all who enter through the gate receive, that enables them to witness Christ's crucifixion and resurrection in them*
**   *No earthy man can judge a spiritual being, if you are spiritual, no earthy man will understand you, or discern what you are saying to them unless God opens their heart to receive.*

John 3:5-8

"Jesus answered, 'Verily, verily, I say to you, **except one be born of water and the Spirit**, he cannot enter into the kingdom of God! That which is born of the flesh is flesh (*hears only the* *voice of the flesh*); and that which is born of the Spirit is spirit (*spiritually discerns or hears the Spirit*). Marvel not that I said to you, you must be born anew. The wind blows where it will, and you hear the voice thereof, but know not where it comes from, and where it goes: so is every one that is born of the Spirit."

Keep in the back of your mind that Jesus as The Christ, is Spirit in mans body and all that He reveals is spiritual. Therefore those who are born into the death, burial, and resurrection of Christ become regenerated in spirit and are become "born anew". The process then begins within them, as far as they will allow it, to crucify the flesh, or denying and disallowing it's control. This can only happen as they continue to present their body as a living sacrifice to God, for Him to work in and through them for His good pleasure.* They have passed through the veil of the flesh, the gate and passed from death into life being conjoined to Christ. This is being born of water and the Spirit. Further on in our sharing of the revelation of the mysteries, we will share more on this in Hebrews. The writer of that letter tells them that if they once get to this point then turn back to their old ways and religious traditions, there is no more salvation for them. Christ cannot be crucified again! Thus answering the age old question of whether or not someone can lose their salvation.

For many this will be a door opener and may be their redemption which leads to salvation that said please read and take to heart the following simple outline of faith.

---

*   *We have heard some people who place themselves on the alter of burnt offerings. How can that be a living sacrifice if the offering is burnt? That's a dead sacrifice!*

The Simplicity of Redemption

Take only this gospel that is found in Genesis 3:15, Hebrews then Romans through Philemon, for the mysteries of God which is known as "the Gospel of God's Grace" opens to us His plan for our redemption, which leads to our salvation. This then requires and releases into your hands the denial of your-self will; renounce the lusts of the flesh; set your affections on things above; call upon God for His Holy Spirit; then to walk by faith, and not by sight; adore the Holy Deity of Father, Son, and Holy Spirit, in Whose image and likeness you were first created; and into Whose Name and Power you have been baptized, not by mans doing but rather the Holy Spirit's to be again the living likeness, and holy habitation, of His Life, Truth, Grace and Light, and Holy Spirit. Look up to Christ, who alone is your Redeemer, your Re-generator, your second Adam and Parental head; look to Him, as truly He is, the Wisdom and Power of God, seated at God's right hand in heavenliest place, giving gifts to men; governing, sanctifying, teaching, and enlightening with His Holy Spirit, all those that are spiritually-minded; who live in faith, and hope, and prayer, to be redeemed from the very nature and power of this evil world. Understand that this Gospel is very simple, but many make it out to be complicated. Only when you have followed the Spirit into this Gospel will you be able to love the Lord your God with all your heart, soul and might or strength and your neighbor as yourselves. Then and only then, can you be a child of God and a follower of Christ.

Not so long ago, I asked God how come I wasn't able to love people like I should. I really didn't care about those who are lost and the unbeliever who call themselves Christian but were like me, not knowing the mysteries and the true gospel of faith. But one day He began to open my eyes and heart to His Love and from that point on, I ache for the salvation of others. The beginning of this book has a section titled "Faith Works through Love". This was given to me as He was changing my heart to truly love Him and my neighbors.

God is Spirit, in Whom we live and move and have your being; He is not there to cause us to be a great scholar, through so much "book learning", but so we turn from evil and love goodness. To manifest His holy presence, power, and life within us. It is His Love and Goodness that must do all for us. When He is the ruling Spirit of our heart, Father, Son, and Holy Spirit, has come into us, and made Their abode within our hearts, and then leads and guides us into all that can be Truth.

Lets take a lesson from one of the minor prophets of the Old Testament to see if we can gain some insight into Israel's blindness.

Hosea 3:1-5

"Then said the LORD unto me, 'Go yet, love a woman beloved of her friend, yet an adulteress, according to the love of the LORD toward the children of Israel, who look to other gods, and love flagons of wine.' So I bought her to me for fifteen pieces of silver, and for an homer of barley, and an half homer of barley: and I said unto her, "Thou shalt abide for me many days; thou shalt not play the harlot, and thou shalt not be for another man:

so will I also be for thee. **For the children of Israel shall abide many days without a king, and without a prince, and without a sacrifice, and without an image, and without an ephod, and without teraphim: Afterward shall the children of Israel return, and seek the LORD their God, and David their king; and shall fear the LORD and his goodness in the latter days."** (emphasis mine)

Notice verses 4 and 5 how Israel shall abide without king, prince, sacrifices, images and without ephods and teraphim. No priesthood whatsoever! We know that since the destruction of the Temple in Jerusalem sometime around 70 AD, sacrifices and priesthood stopped functioning just as is said in these verses. This was done so Israel would stop the adultery and idolatrous practice of worship. It was for them to come to their senses as the prodigal son did in the parable of Jesus in Luke 15 beginning at verse 11, and return to their Father not for his wealth or prestige but for Him only and His love. To love Him and honor Him as His son. With this in mind, why then are the Israelites now gathering and making ready for a new priesthood and rebuilding of the Temple? They are gearing up to do sacrifices again, which will only bring great dishonor to God and great harm to themselves. To all those who oppose this Gospel of Grace brought in and established by Christ, take a look at Psalm 2:9.

This same opposition has worn off on to the Christian religion. I say "religion" because that's what it is, but not to be confused with the Christian Faith that is contained in the Gospel of Grace, the New Covenant. The religion of Christianity is the division and segregation of all the different denominations and religions of the world today, including but not limited to, what some call the "non-denominational, charismatic, full gospel, apostolic, holiness, spirit filled . . . ect." All believing they are the ONE and ONLY ONE. Then we have the Quakers, Amish, Mormons, Catholic, Jehovah's Witnesses, Mennonites, Hutterites and list goes on and on and on. All having come about by the rudiments and doctrines of men . . . . NOT GOD! They all mean well and in their own way love God, but unfortunately they are hearing God, because if they did, they would not devise their own system of worship.

Remember Jesus talking with the woman at the well in John 4? She was a Samaritan, and to the Jews, a dog. So, for Jesus to even be conversing with her, was a vast indiscretion against the Jewish law. But Jesus did not come for some religion, but rather for the souls of all men in all nations. He told this woman that they didn't know what they worshiped. He went on to say that God is Spirit, and is seeking for those who will worship Him in spirit and in truth. How can someone worship God in spirit and in truth if they have no understanding of the truth and what is meant by "in spirit"? I've been in services that were reminiscent of some jungle tribes that worship their gods with rhythmic drumming or chanting which causes the participants to fall into a trance and "herky jerk" all over the place. This they call worshiping in the spirit. But I must ask, "What spirit are they in for this worship?" And I've been in services where everyone was so stoic that I thought they had died right there in the pew. Where does God fit in all this? I know that was an example of one extreme to the other, but even that which is in-between, sad to say, is not proper worship either. To worship God IN spirit and

IN truth, one must be ONE with Him in spirit and truth. Jesus told His disciples that He is THE WAY, THE TRUTH AND THE LIFE. So why then, are we all not worshiping Him in the same manner as He said to? Because of blindness!

In Acts 15 we find Paul being confronted by a sect of the Pharisees that were believers. They said that the Gentile converts had to be circumcised in order to be saved and keep the Law of Moses. Paul and Barnabas went to Jerusalem to meet with the apostles and elders of the Church to discuss this and come to an agreement. James said his only requirement was that they do not eat things sacrificed to idols nor blood and that they remember the poor. Why would the Pharisee believers require such of new believers? Could it be they were still blind to the whole of this gospel? The Gospel of Grace in Christ has no requirements as this.

In the Acts of the Apostles we see signs, wonders, and miracles being performed. This is not what the Gospel of Grace is all about. It is however, about the working of Christ within the apostles, and His wanting to work in and through all believers. First, by bringing the believer into oneness with Himself and bring them to the acceptability of God. The Body of Christ is that called-out group of Gentile and Hebrew believers under Paul's Gospel of Grace.

Israel is blind to the spiritual things that Jesus, in all His ministry is speaking, that of a spiritual kingdom. Not a kingdom as the literalist claim is a future kingdom, but here and now within us, a present reality. If we fail to hear and see this, it is because we remain in our blindness and sin nature. Jesus said that they who have eyes to see and ears to hear what the Spirit is saying, will enter the kingdom. This goes back to Genesis 3:15 and the promise of redemption through the seed. For even the LORD's Passover and Marriage Feast is spiritual and relates back to the killing of the animal to cover the sin of Adam and Eve until the time of the incarnation and the Light causing the birth of Christ within us. Until then that seed remains within the hardness of the shell which is man's heart. This is what Israel did not see. That the bursting forth of that seed by the Light of Christ (which is this Gospel of Grace) was to bring about their total salvation. But, because of their rebellion, God gave the commandments and specific instructions to Moses, for the people to keep them in a corral of sorts until such time as they would be set free in Christ, and be sent as priests to the nations. Now we all know this didn't happen. They continued in disobedience and rebellion which brought about the adultery and idolization of the very law that was to keep them only unto God.

God still has a love that is now not just for Israel as in the beginning, but for all people. God so loved that He gave His only begotten Son for us to become one with and receive Him as our wisdom, righteousness, sanctification and redemption. Israel and all mankind, still has that same opportunity today if they would only come out of their rebellion and disobedience and hear the voice of God calling as He called for Adam in the garden after the fall, and answer by saying, "Yes Lord, be it unto me according to Your Will."

Isaiah59:1-2

"Behold, the LORD's hand is not shortened, that it cannot save, or his ear dull, that it cannot hear; but your iniquities have made a separation between you and your God, and your sins have hidden his face from you so that he does not hear."

Isaiah 59:9-17

"Therefore justice is far from us, and righteousness does not overtake us; we hope for light, and behold darkness, and for brightness, but we walk in gloom. We grope for the wall like the blind; we grope like those who have no eyes; we stumble at noon as in the twilight, among those in full vigor we are like dead men. We all growl like bears; we moan and moan like doves; we hope for justice, but there is none; for salvation, but it is far from us. For our transgressions are multiplied before you, and our sins testify against us; for our transgressions are with us, and we know our iniquities: transgressing, and denying the LORD, and turning back from following our God, speaking oppression and revolt, conceiving and uttering from the heart lying words. Justice is turned back, and righteousness stands far away; for truth has stumbled in the public squares, and uprightness cannot enter. Truth is lacking, and he who departs from evil makes himself a prey. The LORD saw it, and it displeased him that there was no justice. He saw that there was no man, and wondered that there was no one to intercede; then his own arm brought him salvation, and his righteousness upheld him. He put on righteousness as a breastplate, and a helmet of salvation on his head; he put on garments of vengeance for clothing, and wrapped himself in zeal as a cloak."

Matthew 6:21-24

"'For where your treasure is *(whatever that may be)*, there your heart will be also. The eye is the lamp of the body. So, if your eye *(spiritual discerning)* is healthy, your whole body will be full of light, but if your eye is bad, your whole body will be full of darkness. **If then the light in you is darkness, how great is the darkness!** No one can serve two masters, for either he will hate the one and love the other, or he will be devoted to the one and despise the other. You cannot serve God and mammon." (emphasis mine)

Can you see the spiritual meaning here? The light that fills us is to be Christ, indicating the eye that is good. The light that is darkness, indicates that which comes from Satan. Paul tells us that Satan transforms himself as an angel of light, in which he then spews his errors and untruths to the unseeing and therefore unsuspecting. Many believe that the gospel for our final salvation is found in Matthew through John, however it is not. The Gospel of salvation is based on the risen Lord not the ministry of Jesus to Israel. His ministry to Israel was to bring them into repentance and baptism into righteousness, and the kingdom of heaven. They then were to receive the Holy Spirit in Power to become the priesthood to minister to the nations.

Matthew 15:1-14

"Then Pharisees and scribes came to Jesus from Jerusalem and said, "Why do your disciples break the tradition of the elders? For they do not wash their hands when they eat." He answered them, '**And why do you break the commandment of God for the sake of your tradition?** For God commanded, 'Honor your father and your mother,' and, 'whoever reviles father or mother must surely die.' But you say, "If anyone tells his father or his mother, That which you would have gained from me is given to God, he need not honor his father." '**So for the sake of your tradition you have made void the word of God. You hypocrites! Well did Isaiah prophesy of you, when he said:'** "**These people honor me with their lips, but their heart is far from me; in vain do they worship me, teaching as doctrines the commandments of men.**" He called the people to him and said to them, '**Hear and understand: it is not what goes into the mouth that defiles a person, but what comes out of the mouth; this defiles a person.**' Then the disciples came and said to him, "Do you know that the Pharisees were offended when they heard this saying?" He answered, '**Every plant that my heavenly Father has not planted will be rooted up. Let them alone; they are blind guides. And if the blind lead the blind, both will fall into a pit.'**"

Jesus calls the Scribes, Pharisees and Sadducees "blind guides". Paul tells us that we, in this age of grace, are to have knowledge of God's hidden things as well as knowing His will in all things. That as His family we are to be spiritual and imitators of Paul as he is of Christ, which in turn makes us imitators of Christ and having the mind of Christ in all things. This is being heavenly minded not earthly minded. We are to focus on the spiritual things first and foremost and not our earthly possessions and positions.

Matthew 23:16-23

"'Woe to you, blind guides, who say, "If anyone swears by the temple, it is nothing, but if anyone swears by the gold of the temple, he is bound by his oath." 'You blind fools! Which is greater, the gold or the temple that has made the gold sacred?' You say, "If anyone swears by the altar, it is nothing, but if anyone swears by the gift that is on the altar, he is bound by his oath." 'You blind men! Which is greater, the gift or the altar that makes the gift sacred?' 'So whoever swears by the altar swears by it and by everything on it. Whoever swears by the temple swears by it and by him who dwells in it. Whoever swears by heaven swears by the throne of God and by him who sits upon it.' 'Woe to you, scribes and Pharisees, you hypocrites! For you tithe mint and dill and cumin, and have neglected the weightier matters of the law: justice and mercy and faithfulness. These you ought to have done, without neglecting the others.'"

Jesus put these men in their place as they ignored that "law of the first" or "first commandment of importance" and that is to Love God and your neighbor. Jesus uses many parables to bring these and other spiritual truths to the forefront, but many still only seek the gift and not the One who gives the gift. How many can say that they would love the Lord God with all their heart, soul and might it they never received any gift from Him?

Do you love Him, or the gift? Oh, some may say that gifts do not matter, but actions speak so much louder than words. Talk is cheap. If you lost everything that you have worked so hard to gather, all the while telling others that God is the One Who gave them to you, what would you do? How would you handle it? How patient are you in waiting on God? Would you do without something until God brought about? Or would you go out, "stepping out in faith" to make it happen? This is all part of blindness, and many are dying in their sins because of it. They are too stubborn and rebellious to allow themselves to seek the truth in righteousness so the scales fall from there eyes that they may receive there sight.

We must allow scripture to interpret scripture.

2Corinthians 3:12-17, 18

"Since we have such a hope, we are very bold, not like Moses, who would put a veil over his face so that the Israelites might not gaze at the outcome of what was being brought to an end. **But their minds were hardened. For to this day, when they read the old covenant, that same veil remains unlifted, because only through Christ is it taken away.** Yes, to this day whenever Moses is read a veil lies over their hearts. But when one turns to the Lord, the veil is removed. Now the Lord is the Spirit, and where the Spirit of the Lord is, there is freedom. We all, with unveiled face, beholding the glory of the Lord, are being transformed into the same image from one degree of glory to another. This comes from the Lord who is the Spirit." (emphasis mine)

2Corinthians 4:1-7

"Therefore, having this ministry by the mercy of God, we do not lose heart. But we have renounced disgraceful, underhanded ways. We refuse to practice cunning or to tamper with God's word, but by the open statement of the truth we would commend ourselves to everyone's conscience in the sight of God. Even if our gospel is veiled, it is veiled only to those who are perishing. **In their case the god of this world has blinded the minds of the unbelievers, to keep them from seeing the light of the gospel of the glory of Christ, who is the image of God.** For what we proclaim is not ourselves, but Jesus Christ as Lord, with ourselves as your servants for Jesus' sake. For God, who said, 'Let light shine out of darkness,' has shone in our hearts to give **the light of the knowledge of the glory of God** in the face of Jesus Christ. But we have this treasure in jars of clay, to show that the surpassing power belongs to God and not to us." (emphasis mine)

Let us take one more for comparison, found in Ephesians 4:18

Ephesians 4:17-27

"Now this I say and testify in the Lord, that you must no longer walk as the Gentiles do, in the futility of their minds. **They are darkened in their understanding, alienated from the life of God because of the ignorance that is in them, due to their hardness of heart.** They have become callous and have given themselves up to sensuality, greedy to practice every kind of impurity. But that is not the way you learned Christ!—assuming that you have heard about him and were taught in him, as the truth is in Jesus, to put off your old self, which belongs to your former manner of life and is corrupt through deceitful desires, and to be renewed in the spirit of your minds, and to put on the new self, created after the likeness of God in true righteousness and holiness. Therefore, having put away falsehood, let each one of you speak the truth with his neighbor, for we are members one of another. Be angry and do not sin; do not let the sun go down on your anger, and give no opportunity to the devil." (emphasis mine)

It is our prayer that you have seen the blindness of Israel, and that this blindness has entered into the Church also. God kept those things hidden from before the foundation of the world, not from us, but from Satan. He had to keep His plan for our redemption out of sight until the proper time. That time was Christ's crucifixion, resurrection and ascension. The "new thing" spoken of by the prophets in the Old Testament.

There are many areas contained in scripture that we could look at, but I think that we can draw our understanding from what we have here. While Israel has drawn blindness upon its self as a nation, keep in mind that the individual Hebrew is still able to change his mind and have entry into the Grace of God. This is in the same way that we as Gentiles have of entry, and puts both Jew and Gentile on the same level playing field, as there is only One Way to acquire redemption which leads to salvation . . . . through Christ Jesus our LORD!

SUBTLE DECEPTION OF
THE WORLDLY KIND

Most everyone that knows me, knows how much I enjoy watching the British Comedies on PBS. There is one show titled, "Are You Being Served?" about the shenanigans of a group of department store employees.

In one episode, three employees in the men's department are outfitting a gentleman with a sport coat. The gentleman customer asked for a particular size and color, and as it was not available, they proceed to show him something else. The coat they showed him was a larger size, so as he put it on and looked in the mirror, one employee held it in the back to make it appear the proper size. When the gentleman turned around to see the backside of the coat, the employee held it in the front. The gentleman said it felt a bit snug, so the employee told him to take a deep breath in and out. This, of course was a ploy so the customer wouldn't be aware of the deception of its letting it out a bit. When the customer asked about the price, one employee told him it was 30 pounds. He hesitated then said that it was a bit much. Another employee then told the customer, "But it has been reduced to 42 pounds!" the first employee then says, "that's a savings of 12 pounds!" The customer likes what he hears and says that he'll think about it. The three employees then stand looking at him with their arms crossed across their chests, so the customer gives in and takes it. Now, did you catch it? Did you catch the deception? Understanding that this is just a funny storyline, meant throw in a bit of confusion for the customers so the employees can make their commission on sales, this is not unlike the world today. Unfortunately, it's the way of a lot of the teaching of the Word of God as well.

You might call some churches a big box store ministry You know, with the "Blue Light Specials". Customers will literally flock to something they are led to believe is a bargain.

So will people that are not spiritually discerning, flock to see the miracles, signs and wonders, or a so called Christian band play in concert or a prophet, evangelist or teacher that is a good speaker and motivator.

A Christian will gobble up anything they think is of God. Same as shoppers who will not study the regular price of an object to know whether or not it's really on sale. They will gobble it up just because it has a "percent off sale" sticker on it. Having worked in a department store, I've seen this first hand.

Dresses, for example, will arrive with the price tags showing the original price. Let's say that a dress came in at the original price of $100.00. We have the paper work showing that it's already 40% off (making the dress $60.00), so the rack has a percent off sign placed atop it. Not a bad bargain already. A few days later, a sign goes on the rack of and additional 20% off the sale price (bringing the price of the dress to $48.00). Even better. This goes on for a couple weeks until the dress is put on a clearance rack.

Once the dress goes on the clearance rack it then becomes 50% off the original price. You do the math! Subtle deception, unless you watch closely.

Now, mind you not all stores do such things, but I have seen it done. Customers will knock the doors down and trample each other just because they are getting a bargain. Not knowing that they are being "suckered" into actually paying more.

With this in mind, unless someone has an intimately close relationship with the Spirit of God, and has the Spirit of Christ, he/she can be easily deceived by the spirit of this world, or the devil/Satan. Don't think for one minute he won't give you chapter and verse of that Bible, he probably knows it better than you do. But, he will tweak it or twist it ever so slightly, and unless you are spiritually discerning and have seeing eyes and hearing ears, you will fall for his cleverly disguised deception, and will start believing the word says something it does not!

A good example is looking at I Corinthians 12, where the apostle Paul is teaching the Christians in Corinth about the working of the Holy Spirit. If you study you will find that everywhere Paul went, the Jews followed him trying to trip up the ministry of Grace, and making the new Christians believe they have to follow the law as well.

The whole point Paul is making is that the Holy Spirit's power has been given to us for our good. It is God working in us and through us for His good pleasure. We must be totally given over to Him in every way and receptive to His activity in us. This power is to help us in our growth and development as a new spiritually divine creature in Christ. Not so we can go around laying hands on everything that moves and speak "prophetically" like the Old Testament prophets, or whatever. I'm not saying that it is never to be done, but unless we are walking in that maturity of Christ in us, we are just deceiving ourselves.

We must start looking and examining things closer with keener eyes and ears, as the Holy Spirit lead us. Allowing Him to give us the full understanding. We begin to really trip ourselves up when we attempt to gain knowledge mentally of all things. Remember that's were Satan deceived Adam and the woman (later named Eve) by his telling them they could have knowledge of good and evil.

We must be on the alert to the devices of deception. Another being, that there is nothing more than the 66 books of the canonized Bible we know today. Or the King James Version, being the only translation. Well, unless you check them all out, you won't know that the King James is not entirely correct, and that the Old Testament was written in Greek (The Septuagint LXX) and is more correct in some parts than the ancient Hebrew.

I know some people that would fight you to the death over things like this, but unless you are willing to take the blinders off and allow God to guide and direct you into the things He wants you to see and hear, you will never know. Do a bit of homework, check things out for yourself and stop allowing someone else to tell you everything.

Let's say we put a sentence in front of you that actually says, "The wagon is red." Someone is constantly telling you that it doesn't really mean red, but the wagon is more of a pinkish color, and you see the wagon, and yes, it appears pink. After awhile you will believe that red is not red but pink. So then your interruption of that sentence and your visual of the wagon is distorted. Perhaps the wagon does appear a bit pinkish, since it's been faded by the sun, and this is now what is visible. But pink is not it's true color, is it? The color has been diluted because it sat in the sun so long. Now, if you were to go to the manufacturer of that wagon to find the original color, you would find that it was actually red, not pink.

This is a whacky illustration, I know. But think about the word of God and how someone, centuries ago said that a word was translated as one thing but that wasn't entirely correct. Over the years everyone believed it to be true, but it was wrong. Just a slight bit of twisting, whether by accident or true deception can make a whole lot of difference.

So, be TRUE to the One within you and allow Him to show you things you may never have seen before. Don't be afraid of seeing the truth. Satan is the one who will deceive you into thinking that anything you have never heard before is heresy. Check it out for yourself allowing God's Spirit to lead you and guide you into those areas where you have never been before. Allow Him to use that "dunamus" power within you for your growth and maturity. And remember this one thing . . . . we must allow God's character and nature to manifest in our behavior. The physical is one thing, but the spiritual is what matters most . . . . because God is Spirit!

SPEAKING THE WISDOM
OF GOD IN MYSTERIES

"But we speak the wisdom of God in a mystery, the hidden wisdom, which God ordained before the world unto our glory" 1 Corinthians 2:7

How many times have we heard people say that we are not to know the mysteries of God? I used to hear it all the time as a child. I would wonder why we were not to know these mysteries, if God hid them for us, then why shouldn't we know them? Paul says in 1 Corinthians 4:2 and 3 that we are to be stewards of these mysteries and that we are to be found faithful. Or one might say, we are to be full of faith. How can one be full of faith if they don't know the mystery of faith, and how it works? Peter gets in on it also in 1 Peter 4:10 when he says, "As every man hath received the gift, even so minister the same, one to another, as good stewards of the manifold grace of God."

We must know and believe these mysteries, but most of all we must receive them. We can know and believe a lot of things but if we do not receive them as ours, the knowledge is just that, knowledge. Something to take up space in your brain. There is great emphasis on learning and we should learn, but if what we are learning is unnecessary jargon, then we become nothing more than hoarders. Our brain is so cluttered with junk and there is no way to sort it out. But a hoarder will hold on to useless trash rather than throw it out because they believe it will some day be useful.

Don't get me wrong education is important and has it's place. Our daughter and daughter-in-law are both school teachers. They teach the little ones who are in that "sponge" phase (as I call it). They will soak up any and everything they see, so it is very important that they learn from those who are in Christ, so that which they are learning has a base or foundation of righteousness. The public schools have policies against the teachings of Christ, however, they cannot keep it out when the teachers are teaching with love as our Jessica and Sarah do. The way these girls love can only come from One source that is God.

When our Jessica was just a little might of about 5 years old, she would come home from her half day of kindergarten, grab her 2 year old brother Eric sit him down and begin teaching him all she had learned that day. Her desire to teach carried through her childhood. She even, at the age of 11 or12, taught the children in church, to the point that she would study the bible all week, carefully choosing the material suited for the kids. She was made to stop because one man said that it was wrong for a child to teach other children. But that didn't stop her. We had home bible studies for our neighbors and Jessica had her dad fix up a spot in the basement as a little classroom and she gathered the materials needed to teach those babies. Yes, some were not even walking yet! It wasn't until after she married and had children of her own, and they were in school and she was volunteering in the classroom and anywhere else she could, that the principle came up to her and suggested she become a substitute teacher. She thought for a little extra money she would sub a couple days a month. She got so many calls to sub that she was literally working every day of the month. This is when she decided it was time to go back to school to get her teaching credentials. And she did. She is now a 1st grade teacher in one of our local public schools. And I must say, she shines as Christ's Glory shines through her. I shared this to show you how God will provides for those who are willing to do His Will.

If we are willing to do His Will He even provides that burning desire within us to carry it through. We feel as though we will burst if we do not share what He reveals through Christ. It is imperative that we know His Will and the mysteries He has hidden for us. He has not hidden them FROM us but FOR us!

Below you will find scripture laying out the need for the knowledge of these mysteries as well as the mysteries themselves. Please read these slowly and cautiously to hear and see what they are saying.

Ephesians 3:1-12

"For this cause I Paul, the prisoner of Christ Jesus in behalf of you Gentiles, if so be that you have heard of the dispensation of that grace* of God which was given me to you-ward; how that by revelation was made known to me the mystery, as I wrote before in few words, whereby, when you read, you can perceive my understanding in the mystery of Christ; which in other generations was not made known to the sons of men, as it has now been revealed to His holy apostles and prophets in the Spirit; to wit, that the Gentiles are fellow-heirs, and fellow-members of the body, and fellow-partakers of the promise in Christ Jesus through the gospel, where of I was made a minister, according to the gift of that grace of God which was given me according to the working of His power. To me, who am less than the least of all saints, was this grace given, to preach (*proclaim, make known*) to the Gentiles the unsearchable riches of Christ; and to make all men see what is the dispensation** of the mystery which for ages has been hid in God who created all things; to the intent that now to the principalities and the powers in the heavenly places might be made known through the church (*the mystical Body of Christ*) the manifold wisdom of God, according to the eternal purpose which He purposed in Christ Jesus our Lord: in whom we have boldness and access in confidence through our faith IN Him." (emphasis mine)

* *Grace is the benefit or the nature of the benefactor*
** *Dispensation is the dispensing of the truths in the change in directions and of the mysteries that set a new set of responsibilities and directions for behavior in lifestyle, wherein God deals with us all in His fashion.*

Act 9:1-25

"But Saul, still breathing threats and murder against the disciples of the Lord, went to the high priest and asked him for letters to the synagogues at Damascus, so that if he found any belonging to the Way, men or women, he might bring them bound to Jerusalem. Now as he went on his way, he approached Damascus, and suddenly a light from heaven flashed around him. And falling to the ground he heard a voice saying to him,

"Saul, Saul, why are you persecuting me?" And he said, "Who are you, Lord (*Yehovah that is to say Master*)?" And he said, "I am" Jesus, whom you are persecuting. Rise and enter the city, and you will be told what you are to do." The men who were traveling with him stood speechless, hearing the voice but seeing no one. Saul rose from the ground, and although his eyes were opened, he saw nothing. So they led him by the hand and brought him into Damascus. For three days he was without sight, and neither ate nor drank. Now there was a disciple at Damascus named Ananias. The Lord said to him in a vision, 'Ananias.' And he said, "Here I am, Lord." And the Lord said to him, 'Rise and go to the street called Straight, and at the house of Judas look for a man of Tarsus named Saul, for behold, he is praying, and he has seen in a vision a man named Ananias come in and lay his hands on him so that he might regain his sight.' But Ananias answered, 'Lord, I have heard from many about this man, how much evil he has done to your saints at Jerusalem. And here he has authority from the chief priests to bind all who call on your name.'* But the Lord said to him, 'Go, for he is a chosen instrument of mine to carry my name before the Gentiles and kings and the children of Israel.

I will show him how much he must suffer for the sake of my name.' So Ananias departed and entered the house. And laying his hands on him he said, 'Brother Saul, the Lord Jesus who appeared to you on the road by which you came has sent me so that you may regain your sight and be filled with the Holy Spirit.' Immediately something like scales (*the veil that covers all Israel*) fell from his eyes, and he regained his sight. Then he rose and was baptized; and taking food, he was strengthened. For some days he was with the disciples at Damascus. Immediately he proclaimed Jesus in the synagogues, saying, 'He is the Son of God.' All who heard him were amazed and said, 'Is not this the man who made havoc in Jerusalem of those who called upon this name? And has he not come here for this purpose, to bring them bound before the chief priests?' Saul increased all the more in strength, and confounded the Jews who lived in Damascus by proving that Jesus was the Christ. When many days had passed, the Jews plotted to kill him, but their plot became known to Saul. They were watching the gates day and night in order to kill him, but his disciples took him by night and let him down through an opening in the wall, lowering him in a basket." (emphasis mine)

* *Notice Ananias is judging Saul based on "hearsay", we have a tendency to judge what the Word is saying based on what we have heard someone else say about it, what they think it is saying, without checking it out for ourselves and rightly dividing the word with the help of the Holy Spirit.*

Galatians 1:11-18

"For I would have you know, brothers, that the gospel that was preached by me is not man's gospel. For I did not receive it from any man, nor was I taught it, but I received it through a revelation of Jesus Christ. For you have heard of my former life in Judaism, how I persecuted the church* of God violently and tried to destroy it. I was advancing in Judaism beyond many of my own age among my people, so extremely zealous was I for the traditions of my fathers.

But when He who had set me apart before I was born, and who called me by His grace, was pleased to reveal His Son in me, in order that I might preach (*proclaim*) Him among the Gentiles, I did not immediately consult with anyone; nor did I go up to Jerusalem to those who were apostles before me, but I went away into Arabia, and returned again to Damascus. Then after three years (*in Damascus*) ** I went up to Jerusalem to visit Cephas and remained with him fifteen days."

*   *Church: assembly is a better word here. The Jewish-Christians or believers continued to assemble in the synagogues because they were still under the Law, practicing the traditions and customs of their fathers. They had not fully broken off from they're religious customs and traditions.*

**   *Some think that Saul spent only 3 years in Arabia, but looking closely at the position of the words, the 3 years were spent in Damascus before he left for Jerusalem. This is nothing to tell us how much time he spent alone with Christ in the desert of Arabia.*

Act 9:26-31

"When he had come to Jerusalem, he attempted to join the disciples. And they were all afraid of him, for they did not believe that he was a disciple. But Barnabas took him and brought him to the apostles and declared to them how on the road he had seen the Lord, who spoke to him, and how at Damascus he had preached boldly in the name of Jesus (*that He was the Messiah, the King of Israel*). So he went in and out among them at Jerusalem, preaching boldly in the name of the Lord. He spoke and disputed against the Hellenists. But they were seeking to kill him. When the brothers learned this, they brought him down to Caesarea and sent him off to Tarsus. So the church (*the assembly of Jewish believers in a synagogue*) throughout all Judea and Galilee and Samaria had peace and was being built up. And walking in the fear of the Lord and in the comfort of the Holy Spirit, it multiplied." (ESV) (emphasis mine)

We find in some text this word "Hellenists" reads Grecians here. These are Greek speaking Hebrews which are a remnant of the 606 BC scattering of Israel, some text also say that these are non-Jewish people but that is not consistent with historic documents, and the Jewish believers from Jerusalem.

I know there are a lot of scripture here to get through, but please bare with me as scripture interprets scripture. All this needs to be verified so there is no doubt of what it is saying. Each of these passages are revealing mysteries that we all are required to know in order to be witnesses of Christ. We cannot be approved by God to preach if we do not know and understand what it is He wants told. If we merely read the word and pick out certain parts that we think are important, we are only serving ourselves, but if we truly desire to serve God and others we must see it as God intended. Shall we press on?

Acts 15 is Luke's account of the meeting of the council at Jerusalem, between Paul and those converted Jews who were preaching that the Gentile converts needed to be circumcised in order to be saved. They were still so staunch in their Jewishness and were attempting to make the Gentiles give in to their traditions. We see that in the Christians today. They still think that in order to truly be saved they must continue the Jewish traditions, but with a modern twist. God has been searching for men who will minister His plan and purpose today. So, why continue in the historical traditions of the Jews? He found, in

Paul and Barnabas, His revelation would be spread through those who received it.

We see on through Acts 15 that there was great dissension between these groups. The converted Jews who continued in the tradition of Judaism and the one's who had broke free of it and worshiped God in spirit and in truth. After much debate, Peter would stand up and tell them that it had been said that they would hear the word of the gospel by of the mouth of the Gentiles, and they would believe. Their hearts would be cleansed so why are they still putting a yoke of bondage on the necks of the Gentiles by making them abide by the Jewish customs and traditions? The decision came down that the Gentile believers should no longer be troubled, but they did ask that they abstain from things polluted by idols and sexual immorality and to remember the poor.

Paul's account of Acts 15 as see above, can be found in Galatians 2:1-10. In this scripture, Paul relates how he went up to Jerusalem to speak to the council because of a "revelation" given to him by God. He tells them he has been entrusted with the gospel to the Gentiles the same as Peter has been entrusted with the gospel to the Jews. Paul then says this, "and when James and Cephas (Peter) and John, who seemed to be pillars, perceived the grace that was given to me, they gave the right hand of fellowship to Barnabas and me that we should go to the Gentiles and they to the circumcised. Only, they asked us to remember the poor, the very thing I was eager to do."

The secret revealed concerning the gospel can be seen here in Romans 16:25-27 "Now to Him who is able to strengthen you according to my gospel and the preaching of Jesus Christ, **according to the revelation of the mystery*** that was kept secret for long ages past** but has now been disclosed and through the prophetic writings **has been made known to all nations**, according to the command of the eternal God, **to bring about the obedience of faith**—to the only wise God be glory forevermore through Jesus Christ! Amen." (emphasis mine)

* *the seed of Genesis 3:15*
** *The long ages past takes us back before time began to Genesis 1:1 for this was in the heart of God prior to creation.*

Here we see that the revelation of the mystery has been made known to ALL nations. How? Through the power of the Holy Spirit hidden within all men by way of that tiny seed placed in woman in the garden after the fall. Why? To bring about the obedience of faith. And what is that faith? Christ our redeemer is that Faith! It's His Faith within me as He lives His Life through me. Hebrews 11:1 tells us, "Now faith is the substance of things hoped for the evidence of things not seen." What does this mean? The hope given to our forefathers and the prophets. They had no doubt that the Hope was Christ. They never got to see it fully come about but trusted and believed that what God said was so. They could literally "take it to the bank" as it was a done deal. Faith is that substance or the reality of Christ. Now faith is, faith is Christ, Christ is now, Faith is now. Christ IS the substance of that which those of the Old Testament HOPED for. They only saw the shadow of that which was to come, and still they believed and received it. They believed the shadow was the reality to come. This is why, we do not take our doctrine from the Old Testament. We read and study it for the balance of understanding the mysteries and secrets hidden by God, of that which He had instrumented before the foundation of the world.

1Corinthians 2:1-13

"I, when I came to you, brothers, I did not come proclaiming to you the testimony of God with lofty speech or wisdom. For I decided to know nothing among you except Jesus Christ and Him crucified. I was with you in weakness and in fear and much trembling, and my speech and my message were not in plausible words of wisdom, but in demonstration of the Spirit and of power, that your faith might not rest in the wisdom of men but in the power of God. Yet among the mature we do impart wisdom, although it is not a wisdom of this age or of the rulers of this age, who are doomed to pass away. But we impart a secret and hidden wisdom of God, which God decreed before the ages for our glory. None of the rulers of this age understood this, for if they had, they would not have crucified the Lord of glory. But, as it is written, "What no eye has seen, nor ear heard, nor the heart of man imagined, what God has prepared for those who love him"—these things God has revealed to us through the Spirit. For the Spirit searches everything, even the depths of God. For who knows a person's thoughts except the spirit of that person, which is in him? So also no one comprehends the thoughts of God except the Spirit of God. Now we have received not the spirit of the world, but the Spirit (*the ontological essence of Christ*) who is from God, that we might understand the things freely given us by God. We impart this in words not taught by human wisdom but taught by the Spirit, interpreting spiritual truths to those who are spiritual. Now the natural man (*the religious reasoning intellectual*) receives not the things of the Spirit of God: for they are foolishness unto him; and he cannot know them, because they are spiritually judged (*received or understood*)." (ESV) (emphasis mine)

The religious reasoning intellectual is the Pharisee, Sadducee, and scribes along with the lawyers who kept and continue to keep, the Hebrews from knowing God and His revelation by enforcing the rites, rituals and traditions of Judaism. Today we have those who are in the Christian religion, that have gone to educational institutes for higher learning and degrees of man's designs. Thusly, by filling only the intellect, mankind, in many cases, is merely forsaking God and His plan for mankind which is to be a spiritual man known by God.

1Corinthians 4:1-7 is the Stewardship of the Secret;

"This is how one should regard us, as servants of Christ and stewards of the mysteries of God. Moreover, it is required of stewards* that they be found trustworthy. But with me it is a very small thing that I should be judged by you or by any human court. In fact, I do not even judge myself. For I am not aware of anything against myself, but I am not thereby acquitted.** It is the Lord who judges me. Therefore do not pronounce judgment before the time, before the Lord comes, who will bring to light the things now hidden in darkness and will disclose the purposes of the heart. Then each one will receive his commendation from God. I have applied all these things to myself and Apollos for your benefit brothers, that you may learn by us, not to go beyond what is written that none of you may be puffed up in favor of one against another. For who sees anything different in you? What do you have that you did not receive? If then you received it, why do you boast as if you did not receive it?"

*   *Those who hold the principles of Christ*
** *Acquitted: to be set free of a duty or charge, discharge of duty or obligation. In other words; I'm not discharged from my assigned duty.*

1Corinthians 13:1-7 Tells us how Faith works through Love;

"If I speak in the tongues of men and of angels, but have not love, I am a noisy gong or a clanging cymbal. If I have prophetic powers*, and understand all mysteries and all knowledge, and if I have all faith, so as to remove mountains, but have not love, I am nothing. If I give away all I have, and if I deliver up my body to be burned, but have not love, I gain nothing. Love is patient and kind; love does not envy or boast; it is not arrogant or rude. It does not insist on its own way; it is not irritable or resentful; it does not rejoice at wrongdoing, but rejoices with the truth. Love bears all things, believes all things, hopes all things, and endures all things."

*   *The ability to speak (teach and proclaim God's mysteries) by the power of the Holy Spirit, the word of truth.*

Love is putting the other person's interests and well being first and is that which seeks the highest good of others. It is the sacrifice made to find the pearl of great price. It's the willingness to deny and forsake your own desires for the betterment of those God places before you. Within this, comes the understanding of the greatest mystery of all, and the richness which is of Christ, hidden in 1 Corinthians 11.

1 Corinthians 14:1-6

"Pursue love, and earnestly desire the spiritual gifts, especially that you may prophesy*. For one who speaks in a tongue speaks not to men but to God; for no one understands him, but he utters mysteries (*the principles of Christ*) in the Spirit.** On the other hand, the one who prophesies speaks to people for their up building and encouragement and consolation. The one who speaks in a tongue builds up himself, but the one who prophesies (*edifies*) builds up the church. Now I want you all to speak in tongues, but even more to prophesy. The one who prophesies is greater than the one who speaks in tongues, unless someone interprets, so that the church may be built up. Now, brothers, if I come to you speaking in tongues, how will I benefit you unless I bring you some revelation or knowledge or prophecy or teaching?" (emphasis mine)

*   *This word "prophesy" is to preach, proclaim and to teach others the Word or revelation given by God, and not as many attempt to do today which is nothing more than fraudulent fortune telling. Tickling the ears of the listeners to motivate them by telling them things they want to hear.*

**   *We are speaking, praying Gods word back to Him—His word is His will, we are the means through which God has chosen to implement His will on the earth through the body.*

1 Corinthians 15:50-58 Tells of the calling out of the Body of Christ;

"I tell you this, brothers: flesh and blood (*reasoning, intellectual man*) cannot inherit the kingdom of God, nor does the perishable inherit the imperishable. Behold! I tell you a mystery. We shall not all sleep, but we shall all be changed, in a moment, in the twinkling of an eye, at the last trumpet. For the trumpet will sound, and the dead will be raised imperishable (*those in Christ*), and we shall be changed. For this perishable body must put on the imperishable, and this mortal body must put on immortality.

When the perishable puts on the imperishable, and the mortal puts on immortality*, then shall come to pass the saying that is written: "Death is swallowed up in victory. O death, where is your victory? O death, where is your sting?" The sting of death is sin, and the power of sin is the law (*Genesis 2:15-17*). But thanks be to God, who gives us the victory (*the redemption of Genesis 3:15*) through our Lord Jesus Christ. Therefore, my beloved brothers, be steadfast, immovable, always abounding in the work** of the Lord, knowing that in the Lord your labor is not in vain."

---

* *This is a "dualism" hidden in this word. One dealing with 1 Corinthians 11 and the other with 2 Corinthians 6, concerning the fact that once you "come from among them" and "become one with Christ in God" you then become a NEW creature and obtain immorality. The inner man of imperishable immortality is to rule the flesh or that which is perishable, the mortal that will fall away either when called out or in the falling asleep of the body (death of the body).*

** *Work, here spoken of, is the preparing of one's self through prayer and the studying of the word, praying to be ready to move out when He tells you and not before. For this work it requires one to be spiritual as stated elsewhere.*

2 Corinthian 4:1-18 speaks of the Unveiled Gospel;

"Therefore seeing we have this ministry, even as we obtained mercy, we faint not: but we have renounced the hidden things of shame, not walking in craftiness, nor handling the word of God deceitfully; but by the manifestation of the truth commending ourselves to every man's conscience in the sight of God. If our gospel is veiled, it is veiled in them that perish (*because they have chosen not to receive God's Word of Grace*): in whom the god of this world has blinded the minds of the unbelieving, that the light of the Gospel of the Glory of Christ, who is the image of God, should not dawn upon (*within*) them. We preach not ourselves, but Christ Jesus as Lord, and ourselves as your servants for Jesus' sake. Seeing it is God, that said, **'Light shall shine out of darkness'**, who shined in our hearts, to give the **light of the knowledge of the glory of God** in the face of Jesus Christ. But we have this treasure in earthen vessels, that the exceeding greatness of the power may be of God, and not from ourselves; pressed on every side, yet not straitened; perplexed, yet not unto despair; pursued, yet not forsaken; smitten down, yet not destroyed; always bearing about in the body the dying of Jesus, that the **life also of Jesus may be manifested in our body**. For we who live are **always delivered unto death for Jesus' sake, that the life also of Jesus may be manifested in our mortal flesh**. So then death works in us, but life in you.

But having the same spirit of faith, according to that which is written, I believed, and therefore did I speak; we also believe, and therefore also we speak; knowing that He that raised up the Lord Jesus shall raise up us also with Jesus, and shall present us with you.

For all things are for your sakes, that **the grace, being multiplied through the many,** may cause the thanksgiving to abound to the glory of God. Wherefore we faint not; but **though our outward man is decaying, yet our inward man is renewed day by day**. For our light affliction, which is for the moment, works for us more and more exceedingly an eternal weight of glory; while we look not at the things which are seen, but at the things which are not seen: for the things which are seen are temporal; but the things which are not seen are eternal." (emphasis mine)

As you can see, this ties together with what was said earlier. Once the veil is removed, or the scales in Paul's case, the understanding of the mysteries and secrets become clear. All at once you will see it and shout out, "I GET IT!!" What a great and glorious feeling that is! Then all you will be able to do is get on your knees with your hands held high crying out, "HOLY, HOLY HOLY, IS THE LORD GOD ALMIGHTY, WHO WAS AND IS AND IS TO COME!" The warmth of His Grace and Mercy will be streaming down you as though someone poured thick oil on your head. The love that welds up within your being is so strong and powerful toward Him and His Love is returned to you. It then becomes apparent why Jesus said in Matthew 10:37 "He that loveth father or mother more than me is not worthy of me: and he that loveth son or daughter more than me is not worthy of me."

There is no body you could love more than Him. Once you have had your eyes and ears opened to the true Gospel of Christ Jesus, His Grace becomes your all sufficiency, and your every need is met. Because He is your need, all that you need now or ever have needed, or ever will.

Ephesians 1:1-14 The Will of God explained through marriage;

"Paul, an apostle of Christ Jesus by the will of God, to the saints who are in Ephesus, and are faithful in Christ Jesus: Grace to you and peace from God our Father and the Lord Jesus Christ. Blessed be the God and Father of our Lord Jesus Christ, who has blessed us **IN** Christ with every spiritual blessing in the heavenly places, even as He chose us **IN** Him before the foundation of the world (*Genesis 3:15*), that we should be holy and blameless before Him. In love He predestined us for adoption as sons through (***IN***) Jesus Christ, according to the praise of His glorious grace, with which He has blessed (*accepted*) us in the Beloved. **IN** Him we have redemption **through** His blood, the forgiveness of our trespasses*, according to the riches of His grace, which He lavished upon us, in all wisdom and insight **making known to us the mystery of His will**, according to His purpose, which He set forth **IN** Christ as a **plan for the fullness of time**, to unite all things **IN** Him, things in heaven and things on earth.** **IN** Him we have obtained an inheritance, having been predestined according to the purpose of Him who works all things according to the counsel of His will, so that we who were the first to hope in Christ might be to the praise of His glory. **IN** Him you also, when you heard the word of truth, the (this) gospel of your salvation, and believed **INTO** Him, were sealed with the promised Holy Spirit, who is the guarantee of our inheritance until we acquire possession of it, to the praise of His glory."

When Paul says, "In Him" we understand this as the mystery of marriage. The man and woman become one by taking and consummating the vows given and received by both parties.

She then becoming one in him, can do all things in his name or by his authority, just as if he were doing it himself. They have become one flesh, and she is identified with him by his name. She has literally died to her singleness as he has his and they become one. They have not lost their personality or individuality but have become members of each other as one. In other words, we can see each person separately but know that they are one, or "clothed" with each other. The unity of marriage, which is the joining of male and female together as one, is the metaphor of our being baptized into Christ. Christ's side was opened for us to enter into, as the first Adam's side was opened when the essence of woman was removed from his body in Genesis 2:21-24. The baptism into Christ is merely the reverse of the separation of woman from man. In this we are conjoined with Christ. Sharing the same body, we are all many members, but one body. This body has only one head and that is Christ, same a in marriage, there is one head and that is the husband, with his wife at his side. She is his completion as we are Christs. We have received the fullness of the Godhead bodily. Now we understand why our marriage vows say, "what God has joined together, no man can separate" and why Adam said of woman, "flesh of my flesh and bone of my bone" as they became two individual but still one in spirit. Before the fall, Adam and the woman were still divine spiritual beings placed in an earthly body.

*   *Trespasses: past, present, and future deeds*
**   *This plan of God's is not revealed to us as we sit weekly in the institutions of religious ceremonies otherwise known as churches. For it is these ceremonies, that keep man from God, as hindrances to the full Light and Truth of revelation, received as inspirations within the soul and spirit of man.*

Ephesians 3:1-19 Our becoming Heirs with Christ;

"For this reason I, Paul, a prisoner for Christ Jesus on behalf of you Gentiles—assuming that you have heard of the **stewardship of God's grace that was given to me** for you, how the **mystery was made known to me by revelation**, as I have written briefly. When you read this, you can perceive my insight into the mystery of Christ, which was not made known to the sons of men in other generations as it has now been **revealed to His holy apostles and prophets by the Spirit**. This **mystery is that the Gentiles are fellow heirs, members of the same body, and partakers of the promise in Christ Jesus** through the gospel. Of **this gospel** I was made a minister according to the gift of God's grace, which was given me by the working of His power. To me, though I am the very least of all the saints, this grace was given, to preach to the Gentiles the unsearchable riches of Christ, and to bring to light for **everyone** what is the **plan of the mystery hidden for ages in God** who created all things, so that through the church* the manifold wisdom of God might now be made known to the rulers and authorities in the heavenly places. This was according to the **eternal purpose** that He has realized in Christ Jesus our Lord, so I ask you not to lose heart over what I am suffering for you, which is your glory. For this reason I bow my knees before the Father, that according to the riches of His glory He may grant you to be strengthened with power through His Spirit in your inner being, so that Christ may dwell in your hearts through faith (Galatians 2:20)—that you, being rooted and grounded in love may have strength to **comprehend** with all the saints what is the breadth and length and height and depth, and to **know the love of Christ that surpasses knowledge**, that you may be filled with all the fullness of God." (emphasis mine)

* *The Body of Christ, in order to understand these things you have to be a member of the Body, In the Body by faiths receptiveness.*

Ephesians 5:18-33 The revealing of The Mystical Body;

"Do not get drunk with wine, for that is debauchery (Revelation 16:16 through 19:3)*, but be filled with the Spirit, addressing one another in psalms and hymns and spiritual songs, singing and making melody to the Lord **with your heart**, giving thanks always and for everything to God the Father in the name of our Lord Jesus Christ, submitting to one another out of reverence for Christ. Wives, submit to your own husbands, as to the Lord. **For the husband is the head of the wife even as Christ is the head of the church, His body, and is Himself its Savior****. Now as the church submits to Christ, so also wives should submit in everything to their husbands. Husbands love your wives, as Christ loved the church and gave Himself up for her, that He might sanctify her, having cleansed her by the washing of water with the word, so that He might present the church to Himself in splendor, without spot or wrinkle or any such thing, that she might be holy and without blemish.

In the same way husbands should love their wives as their own bodies (Gen 2:21). He who loves his wife loves himself. For no one ever hated his own flesh, but nourishes and cherishes it, **just as Christ does the church, because we are members of His body**. Therefore a man shall leave his father and mother and hold fast to his wife, and the two shall become one flesh. **This mystery is profound, and I am saying that it refers to Christ and the church**. However, let each one of you love his wife as himself, and let the wife see that she respects her husband."** (emphasis mine)

---

*   *Debauchery: habitual lewdness, excessive indulgence of lust, corruption of fidelity which leads to a seduction from duty or allegiance.*

** *The husband is the guardian and protector of the wife as long as she is willingly submitted to him as he is to Christ. As the woman is man's completion we are Christ's completeness filling up the Body of Christ.*

Ephesians 6:10-20 The Spiritual Battle on the Day of Calling Out;

"Finally, be strong in the Lord and in the strength* of His might.** Put on the whole armor of God that you may be able to **stand against** the schemes of the devil. For we do not wrestle against flesh and blood, but against the rulers, against the authorities, against the cosmic powers (*that rule)* over this present darkness, against the spiritual forces of evil in the heavenly places. Therefore take up the whole armor of God that you may be able to **withstand in the evil day**, and having done all, to **stand firm**. Stand therefore, having fastened on the belt of truth, and having put on the breastplate of righteousness, and, as shoes for your feet, having put on the readiness given by the gospel of peace. In all circumstances take up the shield of faith, with which you can extinguish all the flaming darts of the evil one; and take the helmet of salvation, and the sword of the Spirit, which is the word of God, praying at all times in the Spirit, with all prayer and supplication.*** To that end keep alert with all perseverance, making supplication for all the saints, and also for me, that words may be given to me in opening my mouth boldly to proclaim the mystery of the gospel. For which I am an ambassador in chains that I may declare it boldly, as I ought to speak." (emphasis mine)

The battle or warfare is done spiritually, and what Paul is saying here is that it is only by the knowledge of the mysteries revealed to us as our eyes and ears are opened and unveiled. Otherwise we are "wrestling against flesh and blood" because we are trying to battle with our own intellectual knowledge, by using our own bodies to come against spiritual forces. We have no might or power in ourselves to do that.

* *Strength or power: dominion the voluntary submission to His rule and authority*
** *Might: His forcefulness and ability which works in and through Grace when received in faith through Love.*
*** *Supplication: worship, fellowship, union, and intimacy which expresses our love for Him to Him.*

Colossians 1:24-29 Christ in You the Hope revealed;

"Now I rejoice in my sufferings for your sake, and in my flesh I am filling up what is lacking in Christ's afflictions for the sake of His body, that is, the church,* of which I became a minister according to the stewardship from God that was given to me for you, to make the word of God fully known, the mystery hidden for ages and generations but now revealed to His saints.** To them God chose to make known **how great** among the Gentiles **are the riches of the glory of this mystery**, which is **Christ in you, the hope***** of glory. Him we proclaim, warning everyone and teaching everyone with all wisdom, that we may present everyone mature in Christ. For this I toil, struggling with all **His energy** that He powerfully works within me." (emphasis mine)

*   *Church: this is not the same as mentioned in Acts, James, Peter, John, Jude or Revelations, this is by personal revelation speaking of is His Body.*
**   *His called out ones or set apart ones.*
*** *This is the hope that our forefathers of faith had in the Old Testament. This hope has now been seen so it is no longer hope for those IN Christ and His Faith.*

Colossians 2:1-5 We are to have Knowledge of the Mystery of God;

"For I want you to know how great a struggle I have for you and for those at Laodicea and for all who have not seen me face to face, that their hearts may be encouraged, **being knit together in love**, to reach all the riches of full assurance of understanding and the knowledge of God's mystery, which is Christ, in whom are **hidden all the treasures of wisdom and knowledge**. I say this in order that no one may delude* you with plausible arguments.** For though I am absent in body, yet I am with you in spirit, rejoicing to see your good order (*discipline*) and the firmness of your faith in Christ." (emphasis mine)

For us to have this knowledge of the mysteries, we must be willing to give up all of man's religion and teaching by coming out from among them and not being unequally yoked with unbelievers or religionists, and totally trust God in what He wants. His Will, done His Way and in His Time.

*   *Delude: is to deceive, beguile, to turn away from, as a wife turns her back on her husband to pursue another, through vain reasonings of religion and mans imagination.*

**   *Arguments: persuasive words again by way of religion (religare which is Latin, meaning to bind or being bound up), from reasoning known as religion which perverts God's grace and truth. The best example is that of the Hebrew priest's as they argued or reasoned from many points of view the meaning of scripture and did this for hours on end. Remember Jesus did this as a young lad when he was found by his parents at the temple in Luke 2:46.*

Colossians 4:2-6 Here we learn how to Speak the Mysteries;

"Continue **steadfastly in prayer, being watchful in it** with thanksgiving. At the same time, pray also for us, that God may open to us a door for the word, to declare the mystery of Christ, on account of which I am in prison—that I may **make it clear**,* which is how I ought to speak. **Walk in wisdom** toward outsiders,** making the best use of the time. Let your speech always be gracious, seasoned with salt, so that **you may know how you ought to answer each person**." (emphasis mine)

*   *Speaking in words easy to understand that it is God's Word or Him speaking through Christ in you. See also Galatians 2:20*

**   *Outsiders: unbelievers seeing your manner of living (conversation). We are not to avoid outsiders or unbelievers so religions teach.*

2Thessalonians 2:1-12 The Revealing of the Lawless one;

"Now concerning the coming of our Lord Jesus Christ and our being gathered together to Him, we ask you brothers, **not** to be **quickly shaken in mind or alarmed**, either by a spirit or a spoken word, or a letter seeming to be from us, to the effect that the day of the Lord* has come. **Let no one deceive you in any way**. For that day will not come, unless the rebellion comes first, and the man of lawlessness is revealed, the son of destruction, who opposes and exalts himself against every so-called god or object of worship, so that he takes his seat in the temple of God, proclaiming himself to be God. Do you not remember that when I was still with you I told you these things? And you know **what is restraining** him now so that he may **be revealed in his time**. For the **mystery of lawlessness is already at work**. Only He who now restrains it will do so until He is out of the way. Then the lawless one will be revealed, whom the Lord Jesus will **kill with the breath** of His mouth and bring to nothing by the appearance of His coming. The coming of the lawless one is by the activity of Satan with all power and false signs and wonders, and with **all wicked deception for those who are perishing**, because they **refused to love the truth** and so be saved**. Therefore God **sends them a strong delusion,** so that they may believe what is false, in order that **all may be condemned** who did not believe the truth but had pleasure in unrighteousness." (emphasis mine)

The lawlessness is the religions of the world, including the Christian religion full of error. Unwilling to give up their belief and "feel good gospel" which is the deception of Satan as he disguises himself as an angel of light. Just because things happen in church, people believe that it has to be God, and unless you have the Spirit of Christ, His very Essence within you, you are not His and are open to every scheme and wiles of the devil and are as children tossed to an fro by every wind of doctrine.

* *The day of the Lord is the starting of the tribulation period with Gods wrath and judgment on all disobedience, lawlessness, and unbelief.*
** *Saved: through the promised redeemer Christ and His death, burial and resurrection for salvation (Genesis 3:15;1Corinthians15:1-6; Romans10:9-10, 1Thessalonians 4:14)*

1Timothy 3:8-16 Revealing the Church Leader's Requirements;

"Deacons likewise must be dignified, not double-tongued, not addicted too much wine, not greedy for dishonest gain. They **must hold the mystery of the faith** with a clear conscience.* Let them also be tested first *(having come through the crisis);* then let them serve as deacons if they prove themselves blameless. Their wives likewise must be dignified, not slanderers, but sober-minded, **faithful in all things.** Let deacons each be the husband of one wife, managing their children and their own households well *(teaching them the mysteries).* For those who serve well as deacons gain a good standing for themselves and also great confidence in the faith that is in Christ Jesus.

I hope to come to you soon, but I am writing these things to you so that, if I delay, you may know how one ought to behave in the **household of God, which is the church of the living God**, a pillar and buttress of the truth. **Great indeed**, we confess, **is the mystery of godliness**: He was manifested in the flesh, vindicated by the Spirit, seen by angels, proclaimed among the nations, believed on in the world, taken up in glory." (emphasis mine)

* *All servants are to have full knowledge of the mysteries before they can hold office, otherwise they are merely hireling caring nothing about the sheep and only of themselves (John 10:11-16), they have to have*

experienced the way of the cross in their own life before they can become qualified for any office.

When we allow the Spirit of God and the Spirit of Christ full reign in us, our eyes will be opened to see that which God wants revealed to us. We will then wonder how did we not see these things before! How could we have gone so long deceiving ourselves thinking we had a handle on Christianity? We get stuck in the bondage as children of doing the same things our parents did before us. They didn't know so how could they teach us? I stand amazed at the Glory of my LORD and MASTER and His Great Love for me. How can we neglect so great Salvation?

THE KNOWLEDGE OF GOD'S PLAN

I n another section of this book we were dealing with the secrets that had been hidden in God since before the foundation of the world. We need to have knowledge of the beginning as covered in the chapter on "Genesis the Untold Story". Genesis is the foundational book which has the secret of Christ hidden within the very text. This secret remains veiled to the unseeing soul. It is God's Will and Plan that all humanity grow into the True knowledge of Christ. It is to this end we have undertaken the revealing of His Truth which is received in Love, Faith, Grace and Truth as these all have to be at work within us.

All the mysteries that had been revealed to Paul are all tied together to each other and are tied together in Christ at the start of the creation story as originally given to Moses, who passed it down to the sons of Israel. The time Moses spent in the wilderness, God was revealing to him, not only the exodus out of Egypt, but also their entrance into the promised land, which was Christ. They were to enter in to this relationship by way of the physical land. Although they did not have spiritual discerning at that time, they were to trust God for all provision. The got very impatient and decided to do things for themselves their way instead of God's Way.

Israel was warned time and time again not to get mixed up with the paganism of their neighbors, but their hardheartedness, impatience and just plain rebellion, against the known will of God caused Israel's scribes to bring into their writings a corrupted and contaminated language of word symbols of corrupted men added to the script or picture language of the Hebrews. Their language did not stay pure but was perverted ever so slightly. During their captivities they increased in corruption, which seen in the worship of Baalim, Molack, as well as other idol worship. These being added into their temple worship.

The Law and the instructions for the tabernacle, complete with utensils and usages, that were given to Moses for Israel, was purely unadulterated and given for one purpose, and that was to lead them to Christ for salvation. These laws were to keep them IN the way of Christ until He could actually come. They did not see it and still today many eyes are blind to that fact. They focus as Israel did only on the Law itself as salvation and not Christ. They look to the external instead of the Eternal. The priests and scribes all sat around adding to what God had already given them. Thinking they were making it better, they made that yoke heavier and more of a burden, that they were not even able to carry it. In the books of Exodus, Leviticus, Numbers and Deuteronomy we find where the scribes, and the reasoning of man added many man made ordinances and laws of their own. They lost the truth and purpose of God which He had hidden within the original. If we look in Genesis 3:3, we will see where the woman added to the command given by God as to the eating of the tree of the knowledge of good and evil. God told them not to eat of it and she told the serpent that they were not to even touch it. By this action of embellishment, Israel willfully turned its back on their God and His first given Law which was on tablets of stone for their learning, as well as to reveal the true unregenerate nature of man. However they did not see the stoniness of their own hearts. Their prophets warned them over and over about these matters but they, not wanting to hear, killed or imprisoned them.

Within the context of the language of the Old Covenant or Testament, we find many times used the word "everlasting" such as "everlasting covenant", everlasting statute, ect . . . It is then the error comes in because there is no spiritual discerning of these phrases. Israel, not believing God's word and forming their own version, they could not and would not see that the everlasting that was spoken of only meant until the end when Christ, Who is the Everlasting One or sometimes called, The Last of Days, would come in. They refused then and many still do today, to accept the fact that the Old cannot be mixed or blended with the New. This is the parable or metaphor Jesus spoke, of the new wine in an old wineskin and the new patch on the old garment. It just cannot happen. But we see it being done all the while. Still hard hearts refusing to trust God.

When the time of the end of those matters, or the Old Covenant, was upon them they did not recognize it. Their leadership had become so corrupt. Jesus Christ the Federal Head of all creation, the second Adam, of the heirship of David, exercised the rule and dominion that was first given man at creation, proving to them who He was. The One they were told to be looking for. The Prophet who would come in the likeness of Moses but in greater righteousness than he. But they chose to turn their backs on Him, and to the offer of the Kingdom of Heaven that was promised to them in the scriptures. This Jesus proclaimed during His ministry. Because He worked the works of God in accord with the book of Genesis and the Righteousness, Love, Grace and Truth He brought in. The book of Acts records a total of about four or more refusals of this Kingdom as seen with the stoning of Stephen found in Acts chapters 6 through 8:3 and the testimony of Peter. When Acts is truly understood and revealed to the spiritually discerning, we see where it splits from them going solely to the Hebrews to making the offer of the kingdom to the nations or Gentiles, for this is in accord with the first promise spoken to Adam for ALL mankind. For in the second Adam, Christ Jesus, is found the promised seed of woman, that is The Redeemer of all mankind. Through whom all who choose to receive Him, He becomes their Salvation, the need of all needs and our source to receive that which we need. He alone is our ark, just as He was in Noah's ark. God had already prepared the man to go to the Gentiles. This is Saul of Tarsus who is first revealed in Acts 7:58, 8:3 and 9. Saul was a stern Pharisee, a lawyer set to argue any law and had received a letter of permission to bind up those who were of The Way. The new converted believers were very fearful of him. Then that day, Christ our Lord met him on that road to Damascus and literally knocked him on his backside! From that point on, his name became Paul and he went about proclaiming the secrets and mysteries of Christ. The reality of the ending of the Old Covenant and the instituting the New Covenant is something the Jews could not nor would not stand for or accept. Still to this day many people, including Christians do not accept it. They continue to blend the two in total rebellion to God. This is lawlessness pure and simple. God made the way and man kicks his heels up not wanting to follow, which is what Jesus told Paul he could not do and that was to "kick against the goad" or pricks of your conscience.

Peter, as chief or lead person of the disciples of the Lord, stayed in Jerusalem along with the others and did not have the mind set required for the change. They were unwilling to fully accept the change that God was bringing about. Although Peter was made privy to it, as we see in Acts chapter 10, when he was shown the sheet with all the food that God said was good to eat, but Peter being a faithful Jew, said he could not eat of that which was unclean. God then told him that He had made it clean and good to eat. Then He told him to go to the home of the Gentile Cornelius. God was setting Peter up for the action found in Acts chapters 22 through 23:11. God's plan is the revealing of redemption through Grace that is the finished work of the cross of Christ Jesus, and is now to be opened to all mankind. Because of the vow He made to Adam in Genesis 3:15.

Jesus is the Christ, Yehovah El, The One Who passed through the gate, as revealed in the Psalms and the Prophets. Putting to death mans sin nature contained within this veil of flesh and thereby opening the entrance to the promised eternal life. Taking the old or ancient path found in Jeremiah 6:16, the path which requires, that the sin nature, contained in the flesh, must die for man to become a divine being again. However, Jesus was without sin. When the natural body or flesh of man dies, his body sees decay or corruption and returns to the earth from which he was taken. The body of Jesus did not see this decay or corruption, but was raised incorruptible as the divine being of original Adam. This action is to show us that through His resurrection and ascension He is reversing that which happened in the garden with Adam at the fall. Adam, in his disobedience of eating the forbidden fruit of the tree of the knowledge of good and evil, caused his body to become corrupt through his spiritual death and subjection to the curse placed on the ground. The same condition that man is in today that has not willfully placed himself, by faith, on that cross of death to this life and received within himself, the Life of Christ to be lived in and through him.

As the high priests of the Old Covenant presented sacrifice yearly to take away the sins of the people of Israel, He, Jesus was raised from the position of a prophet to the position of High Priest after the order of Melchizedek, also that of Apostle, and then confirmed to be the Son of God by His resurrection thusly He then became Christ (LORD and MASTER) Jesus. His blood seals those who are willing to take the same course as He did, by faith and trust, in order to become sons of God and heirs of the promise given to Adam and then to Abram, that being eternal life. The promise of this life eternal is that which caused Abram and Sarai to believe God wholeheartedly. This kind of trust was credited as faith which resulted in righteousness. This caused God to change their names, to reflect this trusting faith and their bodies were regenerated or renewed to enable them to bring forth the son of promise, Isaac.

Whereby those who would so choose of their own free will to enter, would pass into regeneration just as He (Jesus) did. To be joined within Him by baptism into union with and conjoined to, by the action of the Holy Spirit, a working of God and not of man. Being made to sit with Christ at the Fathers right hand in the heavenly place. Whereby re-establishing the ancient path that had been revealed to Moses, but was lost through the corruption of the language, with the exception of the few that walked in righteousness, spoken of Hebrews 11 and Luke 3.

This is the gate of man's redemption, through the death of the nature of the beast into which man had fallen and which he cannot escape on his own. He is tightly chained to death and destruction by, and with his enemy, although Christ Jesus broke the chain that held man. Many do not know that they have been set free from this bondage of sin and death, because they have no understanding of the spiritual discerning necessary to see this freedom. Why? Because they are of the opinion that they have to work in some way to earn their freedom, they are under the veil of blindness which they choose to keep. They are blinded just as Israel was and is even to this day because of a hardness of heart forged in them and upon them by Satan through his system of false teaching, and deception called religion. In these religious practices, they are merely clinging to nothing more then the shadowy figures which were only meant to lead them to the revelation of Christ and His coming operation to set them free. When they realize these are mere shadows of that to come and accept the Truth or Reality and not just the shadow, they then are set free from the bondage of religion and the chains fall off. There is no understanding if the bible is read only with the mental capacity. Even the words which are meant to bring life from death are perverted and distorted through this practice of common usage of language. The Spirit gives Life, but the letter kills.

Romans 16:25-27

"Now to him that is able to establish you according to my gospel and the preaching of Jesus Christ, **according to the revelation of the mystery** which has been kept in silence through times eternal, but **now is manifested**, and by the scriptures of the prophets, **according to the commandment** of the eternal God, is **made known unto all the nations** unto obedience of faith: to the only wise God, through Jesus Christ, to whom be the glory for ever. Amen." (emphasis mine)

We see here in this scripture that the revelation of the mystery has already been revealed, or brought out of hiding, to those who, as Jesus said, "have eyes to see and ears to hear". Without this spiritual discerning there is no knowledge of God or His Will and Plan. Continuing on we must find God's plan for all mankind and this we can find here.

1 Corinthians 2:1-16 God's Plan revealed;

"I, when I came to you, I did not come proclaiming to you the testimony of God with lofty speech or wisdom of men, but rather I decided to know nothing among you except Jesus Christ and Him crucified. I was with you in weakness and in fear and much trembling, and my speech and my message were **not in plausible words of wisdom**, but in **demonstration of the Spirit and of power**, that your faith might not rest in the wisdom of men but in the power of God. Yet among the mature we do impart wisdom, although it is not wisdom of this age or of the rulers of this age, who are doomed to pass away. But we impart **a secret**

and hidden wisdom of God, which God decreed before the ages for our glory. None of the rulers of this age understood this, for if they had, they would not have crucified the Lord of glory. But, as it is written, 'What no eye has seen, nor ear heard, nor the heart of man imagined, what God has prepared for those who love Him'—these things God has revealed to us through the Spirit. For the Spirit searches everything, even the depths of God. For who knows a person's thoughts except the spirit of that person, which is in him? So also no one comprehends the thoughts of God except the Spirit of God. Now we have received not the spirit of the world, but the Spirit who is from God, that we might **understand the things freely given us by God**. We impart this in words **not taught by human wisdom but taught by the Spirit, interpreting spiritual truths to those who are spiritual**. Now the natural man receives not the things of the Spirit of God: for they are foolishness to him; and he cannot know them, because they are spiritually judged (*perceived, concluded, understood*). But he that is spiritual judges (*understands*) all things, and he himself is judged (*understood by*) of no man. For who has known the mind of the Lord, that he should instruct him? But we have the mind of Christ."

Put in simple words this scripture is telling us that God wants all men to have the spiritual discerning to understand Him and His Ways. Mankind is to walk in the same divine unity that Adam did originally and that Jesus had with the Father in His ministry here on earth. We must depend totally on God's operation within us. We must say as Jesus did, "I can do nothing of myself", we must only say and do what we hear the Father say. His power must be at work in us, not us attempting to do things on our own. We can never fill our minds with the knowledge of God, through books or teachings. That will only allow us to know OF Him. Only the Spirit can know the deep things of God, then reveal it to our spirit. Only our spirit must be prepared to receive it, otherwise it goes unknown.

Ephesians 2:14-18

"For he is our peace (*as our Redeemer*), **who made both one**, and broke down the middle wall of partition, having **abolished in the flesh** the enmity, which is **the law of commandments contained in ordinances**; that He might **create in Himself of the two, one new man**, so making peace; and might **reconcile them both in one body to God** through the cross, having slain the enmity thereby:* He came and preached peace to you that were far off, and peace to them that were nigh: for through (IN) Him we both have our access in one Spirit to the Father."

God's plan was to break down that which is between Himself and man, the flesh. The law of commandment contained in ordinances was instituted on behalf of man to keep him, if you will, contained within that certain structure similar to a corral of sorts, until such time that Christ would come to release mankind from the hostility of Satan that separated them. The only place Satan could get to infiltrate was man's flesh which includes his mind. This hostility and enmity includes resentment. Man sometimes resents as well as resists God's Ways. We resent being told that what we believe is wrong and therefore will fight tooth and nail to find a way to force what we believe to fit into God's Plan, as if He needed our help. We are "hell bent" on proving the spiritual things we are told as incorrect. All the while, God's loving Mercy continues to bring them to us in hope of our finally coming to ourselves as the Prodigal son did and we will return home to our Father. If we do not release this resentment and bitterness, it will eat us up alive and cause us to be lost forever.

*   *The enmity or hostility that was contained in the flesh must be crucified by faith in Christ on the cross and kept in this death state, or put to death daily.*

Christ Crucified;

Paul does not rehearse Israel's history; except to make a strong point for our understanding and learning. Many of today, Israel included, stay in the historical past, and thereby remain under the veil as shown in 2 Corinthians chapter 4. This is also the cause of Israel's blindness Paul refers to in Romans 11:25 and in Ephesians 4:18. It's also the cause for the church of today to be lead astray by the spirit of the world along with Israel. There is not a lot of the cross of Christ or the death of Christ rehearsed in truth today, many want to push it aside. In fact many want to remove all reference to the cross and the blood out of the modern Bible all together. They have a liberal and literalistic theology which Paul and the others labeled "another gospel" in their day, of which there are many "gospels today. They also would remove all of the letters of Paul from the Bible if they could; many refuse to use anything of Paul's teachings and even have said that they are heresy and warn their followers to stay away from them altogether. Which as we will find out is a great error and makes those people enmity to God and enemies of the Blood and Cross of Christ and they become His footstool.

1Corinthians 15:1-8

"Now I would remind you, brothers, of **the gospel I preached** to you, which **you received**, in which **you stand**, and **by which you are being saved, IF** you **hold fast** to the word I preached to you—unless you believed in vain. For I delivered to you as of first importance what I also received: that **Christ died for our sins in accordance with the Scriptures, that he was buried, that he was raised on the third day** in accordance with the Scriptures, and that he appeared to Cephas, then to the twelve. Then he appeared to more than five hundred brothers at one time, most of whom are still alive, though some have fallen asleep. Then he appeared to James, then to all the apostles. Last of all, as to one untimely born, he appeared also to me." (emphasis mine)

Paul considers himself to be like a premature baby, born ahead of it's time, when he used the term "untimely born". He was the chief, or first, to receive Christ by way of personal revelation, born again from above into new life in Christ. Paul tells us to be imitators of him as he is of Christ, by receiving the personal revelation of God in Christ, and the only way to do this is by faith, going through the death, burial and resurrection of Christ. Otherwise, we are no different that the Jews who refused to accept this path.

Galatians 3:8-9

"**The scripture** foreseeing that God would justify the Gentiles by faith, **preached the gospel** beforehand **to Abram**, saying, **"In you shall all the nations be blessed."** So then, those who

are of faith are blessed along with Abraham, the man of faith."
(emphasis mine)

The Abrahamic covenant was the building block of what was
to come. The ultimate outcome is to be a family for God of
faithful believers. Children of divine beings as Adam was in
the beginning. That will not happen if we only focus on historic
Israel. The nation of Israel was the prototype of that which was
to come through them, but they stuck their noses up, flipped their
fingers at and turned their backs on God. So, God had to go to
those who would accept His offer of full redemption leading to
salvation and eternal life. This is to be done by becoming that
spiritual being again.

Romans 10:4-13

"Christ is **the end of the law for righteousness** to everyone who
believes. For Moses writes about the righteousness that is based
on the law, that the person who does the commandments shall
live by them. But the **righteousness based on faith** says, 'Do
not say in your heart, Who will ascend into heaven? (That is, to
bring Christ down) or who will descend into the abyss? (That
is, to bring Christ up from the dead).' But **what does it say**?
'**The word is near you, in your mouth and in your heart**';
because, if you confess with your mouth that Jesus is Lord and
believe in your heart that God raised him from the dead, you will
be saved. For with the heart one believes and is justified, and
with the mouth one confesses and is saved.* For the Scripture
says, "Everyone who believes in him will not be put to shame."
For there is no distinction between Jew and Greek; for the same

Lord is Lord of all, bestowing his riches on all who call on him. "Everyone who calls on the name of the Lord will be saved."

To "call upon", is to enter into or take to one's self the Name of the person of Christ Jesus, as a woman takes on or enters into the name of her husband in marriage. To believe "in", "into", "through", "with", "in union with" are all positional words meaning placement, the invisible, unseen reality of a location. Now faith, is that very substance of that thing hoped for. Faith is the reality or evidence which the ancients hoped for but never obtained, we now possess. Our faith is the reality of our being in Christ, the very force or power of the resurrection. That mighty force and power that raised Jesus from the dead is now the faith that is residing within us that unites us in God with Christ. We now walk by or in, this faith and not by sight or the dependency of our five senses. This is the meaning of being spiritually alive, renewed or restored to our original state (Gen 1:27, 2:7, 21-23).

*   *This is unadulterated faith and trust that the heart has. Not to be confused with a knowledge of the mind or intellect, but the absolute giving up in trust, everything to God as Jesus did as the Son of Man. The confession with the mouth is not just repeating something that someone else has said, but the mouth is to speak what the heart contains.*

Romans 6:3-11

"Know you not, (*do you not understand*) that so many of us as were baptized into Jesus Christ (*to be conjoined*) were baptized into his death? Therefore we are buried with him by baptism into (*His*) death: that like as Christ was raised up from the dead by the glory (*power*) of the Father,* even so we also should walk

in (*this same*) newness of life. For if we have been planted **
together in the likeness of his death, we shall be also in the
likeness (*conjoined, into new life*) of his resurrection: knowing
this, that our **old man is crucifie**d with him, that the **body of sin
might be destroyed**, that henceforth we should not serve sin.***
For he that is dead is freed from sin. Now **if we be dead with
Christ**, we believe that **we shall also live with Him**: knowing
that Christ being raised from the dead dies no more; death has no
more dominion over Him. For in that he died, he **died unto sin
once**: but in that he lives, he **lives unto God**. Likewise reckon
you also yourselves to be dead indeed to sin, but alive to God
through (***IN***) Jesus Christ our Lord." (emphasis mine)

*   *Jesus put His trust in the faithfulness of this resurrection power of God
      and this is too, we do, if indeed we are IN Christ. We place out trust in
      Christ's faith, that He has in God's faithfulness.*
**   *See John 12:24, the seed Jesus spoke being.*
*** *or be in bondage to the sin and death of the flesh*

1Corinthians 1:22-25, 27 The Spirit and of Power;

"Seeing that Jews ask for signs, and Greeks seek after wisdom:
but we preach Christ crucified, to the Jews a stumbling block,
and to Gentiles foolishness; but **to them that are called**, both
Jews and Greeks, **Christ the power of God, and the wisdom
of God** . . . . Because the foolishness of God is wiser than men;
and the weakness of God is stronger than men. God uses the
foolish (*or simple things*) of the world to confound the wise of
the world." (emphasis mine)

1Corinthians 1:18-21

"The **word of the cross** is to them that perish foolishness; but to us who are saved it **is the power of God**. For it is written, **I will destroy the wisdom of the wise, and the discernment of the discerning will I bring to naught**. Where is the wise? Where is the scribe? Where is the disputer of this world? Has not **God made foolish the wisdom of the world**? For seeing that in the wisdom of God, the world through its wisdom knew not God, it was God's good pleasure through the foolishness of preaching to save them that believe." (emphasis mine)

Those who spend massive amounts of time gathering knowledge and what they believe to be wisdom, and relying on the discerning and discernment of that knowledge, God says are foolish. The wise men filled with intellectualism is nothing in God's eyes. Many spend hours on seeking truth, but they seek it in the wrong places. They look to the things of historical Israel, through the timelines, genalogy, feast days and offerings, ect . . . all of which God has said is foolishness and will keep them in their sin. They are unable to come to the marriage feast of the Lamb because of the stumbling blocks they themselves have laid in their path.

Romans 1:4, 16-19

"Who was **declared** to be the Son of God **with power**, according to the spirit of holiness, by the resurrection from the dead; Jesus Christ our Lord,—For I am not ashamed of the gospel: for it is the **power of God to salvation** to every one that believes; to the Jew first, and also to the Greek. For therein is **revealed a righteousness of God from faith to faith**: as it is written, **"But the righteous shall live by faith."** For the **wrath** of God is **revealed** from heaven **against all ungodliness and unrighteousness of men, who hinder the truth in unrighteousness**;* because that which is known of God is manifest in them; for God manifested (*revealed*) it to them." (emphasis mine)

*   *Or BY their unrighteousness*

1Timothy 1:9-11

"Knowing this, that the law is not made for a righteous man, but for the lawless and disobedient, for the ungodly and for sinners, for unholy and profane, for murderers of fathers and murderers of mothers, for manslayers, for whoremongers, for them that defile themselves with mankind, for menstealers,* for liars, for perjured persons, and if there be any other thing that is contrary to sound doctrine; according to the glorious gospel of the blessed God, which was committed to my trust."

Although our subject is on the power of the Spirit, we see here in 1 Timothy that the law was designed to keep those of unrighteousness within a certain perimeter of justice or morality. When we come into Christ the power of the Spirit causes the change within us of a new creature. We are under the rule and reign of Almighty God and no longer under the power of the god of this world. Although we live in this world and still must abide by the law of the land, and continue to stop at stop signs, ect . . . however, we are not under the law as Israel was or under the strict disciplines of other religions. We have been set free in Grace, but Grace is not a license to do whatever we desire.

* *One who unjustly reduces free men to slavery under the yoke of mans corrupt religion*

2Thessalonians 2:8-10

"Then the lawless one* will be revealed, whom the Lord Jesus will kill with the breath of his mouth and bring to nothing by the appearance of his coming. The coming of the lawless one is by the activity of Satan with all power and false signs and wonders, and with all wicked deception for those who are perishing, because they refused to love the truth and so be saved."

To love the truth and seek after it in a sense of desperation is to have the Love which is all Truth and Grace restored within us. If He is not so acknowledged as Truth, Grace and Love, then those who call themselves Christian, by the very act of continuing in the rituals of religion, do not have the Spirit of Christ and will not be able to confess Him as their LORD! We see this in Romans 8:9 **"But you are not in the flesh, but in the Spirit, if so be that the Spirit of God dwell in you. Now if any man have not the Spirit of Christ, he is none of his."** It may be that the Christian is born again having the Spirit of God to quicken and make alive his spirit, however it does not stop there! As this book is about progressive revelation, the new convert should never stop progressing in his or her spiritual growth and development. Those who do not have the Spirit of Christ for this growth and development, may continue being involved in their congregations by teaching Sunday School, or some other studies, but sadly they are just like unborn fetuses in a jars of formaldehyde lining the walls of some laboratory somewhere. That may be a gross analogy, however there has to be a punch in the face to get the attention of some. God is not playing church with anyone, so just to be going to church or even being involved is not your entrance into the kingdom.

*   *Some translations use the word "wicked"*

Galatians 6:14-15

"Far be it from me to glory, save in the cross of our Lord Jesus Christ, through which the world has been crucified to me, and I to the world. For neither is circumcision anything, nor uncircumcision anything, **but a new creature**." (emphasis mine)

It is the desire of God that all humanity come to the knowledge of the mystery hidden in God. This mystery is the work of Christ's suffering as the Son of Man, His being our substitute on that tree as the cursed man. It is the new creature of the inward man, of the heart, made flesh or the circumcision of the sin nature that it contained, that is the gate through which all men must enter. This gate through which Jesus entered first, and we as sons of man are to enter as well, is the death of the flesh by Faith, Death to sin and Life anew in God. This therefore, is the restoration or healing that Jesus came to give us.

Philippians 3:8-11

"Yes, verily, and I count all things to be loss for the excellency of the knowledge of Christ Jesus my Lord: for whom I suffered the loss of all things, and do count them but refuse, that I may gain Christ, and be found in Him, not having a righteousness of mine own, or that which is of the law, but that which is through faith in Christ, the righteousness which is from God by faith: that I may know Him, and the power of His resurrection, and the fellowship of His sufferings, becoming conformed to His death; if by any means I may attain to the resurrection from the dead."

The only way mankind can overcome the spirit of sin and death within himself is through death. Now I'm not saying man must kill himself, that is kill his flesh, but this death must happen. The destroying of mans slavery to this sin nature and all sorts of evil, is the gate by which he enters the new Life in Christ. Man is self-sufficient in many ways, such as working for a living to care for his family. This he must, but when it comes to his salvation, he still wants to work for it. This he cannot do. Part of our death is to give up trying to gain our salvation by works of the flesh, through religious practices or performance laws. It is this death of our own self sufficiency that God requires of us all. The entry through the gate and the circumcision or the breaking of His seed in us leads us to newness of Christ's life.

Galatians 2:20

"I have been crucified * with Christ. It is no longer I who live, but Christ who lives in me. The life I now live in the flesh

I live by faith in the Son of God, who loved me and gave Himself for me."

* *To extinguish and subdue selfishness*

Galatians 5:24

"Those who belong to Christ Jesus have crucified the flesh with its passions and desires."

Romans 6:4-7

"We were buried therefore with him by baptism into death, in order that, just as Christ was raised from the dead by the glory (*power*) of the Father, we too might walk in newness of life. We have been united with Him in death like his; we shall certainly be united with Him in a resurrection (*in regeneration in sanctification*) like His. We know that our old self was crucified with him in order that the body of sin might be brought to nothing, so that we would no longer be enslaved to sin. For one who has died has been set free from sin." (emphasis mine)

Now listen carefully to the following . . .

John 1:10-13 The Power and Wisdom of God;

"He was in the world, and the world was made by him, and the world knew him not. He came unto his own, and **his own received him not. But as many as received him, to them gave**

he power to become the sons of God, even to them that believe on his name: Which were born, not of blood, nor of the will of the flesh, nor of the will of man, but of God." (emphasis mine)

We pray for the power of God for many things. We desire to perform signs, wonders and miracles. We want His power to overcome sickness, disease and the devil. But how many pray for His power to BECOME A SON? This power is given freely to those who are willing to be willing to give their lives for His. It's not some game to play, it's the power to be translated from one spiritual kingdom to another. As Paul said in one letter concerning adultery, that for a person to be free to belong to another, the spouse of that person must be dead. Otherwise they commit adultery. Adultery is not what we believe it to be. True adultery is giving your heart to someone when you are married to someone else. Mostly we believe it to be sexual fornication, but it's much deeper than that. To give your heart or love to another you must be free to do so only by the death of your current spouse. Same goes with the spiritual kingdoms. Before we can give our heart wholly to God, we must be free by death, from Satan's realm or kingdom. This is true also of the treasures of our hearts. There are things we become so enamored with such as money, sports, cars, houses, careers and the list goes on and on. Jesus told His disciples that wherever and whatever their treasure is, their hearts will be there with that treasure. Where is my heart? What is my treasure? These are questions we probably need to ask ourselves. As well as, are we willing to pay the price or cost of losing that treasure to have our heart transferred from it to Christ? Such is the meaning of serving two masters . . . you will love one, and begin to hate the other. You will be willing to serve one, and turn you back on the other.

Romans 15:18-21

"I will not dare to speak of any things save those which Christ wrought through me, for the obedience of the Gentiles, by word and deed, in the power of signs and wonders, in the power of the Holy Spirit; so that from Jerusalem, and round about even to Illyricum, I have fully preached the Gospel of Christ; yes, making it my aim so to preach the Gospel, not where Christ was already named, that I might not build upon another man's foundation; but, as it is written, "They shall see, to whom no tidings of Him came, and they who have not heard shall understand."*

* Isaiah. 52:15, 65:1

Galatians 1:10-12

"For am I now seeking the favor of men, or of God? Or am I striving to please men? If I were still pleasing men, I should not be a servant of Christ. For I make known to you, as touching the Gospel which was preached by me, that it is not after man. For neither did I receive it from man, nor was I taught it, but it came to me through revelation of Jesus Christ."

1Corinthians 4:20

"The kingdom of God is not in word, but in power."

Mark 10:27

"Jesus looking upon them said, with men it is impossible, but not with God: for all things are possible with God."

These scriptures all confirm the witness of the power that is God. It is His power alone that will change man's heart and life. There is nothing we can do except to see ourselves as He sees us and become humble and accept His Will to be done His Way. We cannot perform our way into this new life in Christ, nor through observance of Sabbaths, new moons and the like. In fact, our worship of God can only be done in spirit and in truth as Jesus stated to the woman at the well. These are the ones that God is seeking for. No where in scripture do we see God requiring us to worship Him in any particular fashion, in order to become His child. We can do nothing of ourselves! It's all done by the Power of God!

Deuteronomy 32:39

"See now that I, even I, am he, and there is no god with me: I kill, and I make alive; I wound, and I heal; and there is none that can deliver out of my hand."

When you have passed through death into life no one can take you out of His hand or His power.

1Samuel 3:1-10

"The child Samuel ministered to Yehovah before Eli. The word of Yehovah was precious in those days; there was no frequent vision. It came to pass at that time, when Eli was laid down in his place, and the lamp of God was not yet gone out, and Samuel was laid down to sleep, in the temple of Yehovah, where the ark of God was; that Yehovah called Samuel; and he said, Here am I. He ran to Eli, and said, here am I; you called me. He said I called not; lie down again. He went and laid down. Yehovah called yet again, Samuel. Samuel arose and went to Eli, and said, here am I; you called me. He answered, I called not, my son; lie down again. Now **Samuel did not yet know Yehovah, neither was the word of Yehovah yet revealed to him**. Yehovah called Samuel again the third time. He arose and went to Eli, and said, here am I; you called me. **Eli perceived that Yehovah had called the child**. Therefore Eli said to Samuel, Go, and lie down: and it shall be, **if He calls you, that you shall say, Speak, Yehovah; for your servant hears**. So Samuel went and laid down in his place. Yehovah came, and stood, and called as at other times, Samuel, Samuel. Then Samuel said, Speak; for your servant hears." (emphasis mine)

Have you ever been doing something or just in bed sleeping, and hear you name being called? Many people have and think nothing of it, or the get frantic thinking it's paranormal or something of the sort! When one hears their name being called, it's God calling Adam as He did in the garden after the fall. God knows His man Adam, and until we become as Adam was, He doesn't know us. Sound strange? I guess it would since we are all told that God knows us all, but with the mystery of His Wisdom revealed, we will understand this as truth. We hear God calling Adam, but we hear our given name. This is the call to come into His kingdom. Wisdom will tell us first though, that we must "come out from among them". Who? Who are we to come out from among? The religious, unbelievers and disbelievers. Disbelievers? What does that mean? Well, simply that there are those that may believe in God, but not INTO Him and totally DISBELIEVE This Gospel of Christ! As the Lord said those who have ears to hear and eyes to see shall become great in the Kingdom of God. It is His power that we hear calling us to come into His Power and Glory.

1Corinthians 3:6-9

"I planted, Apollos watered; but God gave the increase. So then neither is he that plants anything, neither he that waters; but God that gives the increase. Now he that plants and he that waters are one: but each shall receive his own reward according to his own labor. For we are God's fellow-workers: you are God's husbandry, God's building."

I can only give you His Word as He gives it to me . . . that's planting. Apollos confirms that Word in what he gives you from God . . . that's watering. God is the only One that can cause it all to grow within you, by His power. This is all done for our spiritual learning and increase in knowledge as a new believer in God. Remember, He gives us the power to go from just a new believer to becoming a son. It, this power, is given to those who have entered the gate, of death to the flesh, along with the power to witness to the Truth of God and the resurrection of Christ's Spirit in them again, or as Adam in the beginning.

Acts 16:14

"A certain woman named Lydia, a seller of purple of the city of Thyatira, one that worshiped God, heard us: **whose heart the Lord opened to give heed to the things which were spoken** by Paul." (emphasis mine)

Lydia was willing to be receptive to the strange things that were being said. This is how her heart could be opened by God. We keep the doors closed and locked to our hearts by our stubborn disbelief of the things of God. We may believe in God, that He exists, and love Him to the best of our own ability. However, it's disbelief in these strange things we hear, that slams shut and locks these doors. Man, especially religious man, is resistant to change.

2Corinthians 4:7-11

"We have this treasure in earthen vessels, that the **exceeding greatness of the power may be of God**, and not from ourselves; we are pressed on every side, yet not straitened; perplexed, yet not to despair; pursued, yet not forsaken; smitten down, yet not destroyed; always bearing about in the body the dying of Jesus, that the life also of Jesus may be manifested in our body. For we who live are always delivered to death for Jesus' sake, that the life also of Jesus may be manifested in our mortal flesh." (American Standard Version) (emphasis mine)

We will go through many crisis in our lives here on earth. Those who are God's, and vessels for Christ to live His Life through, can count on it as Paul did. We can be persecuted in so many ways, but God will not allow us to be destroyed. This we too can count on. Paul tells us to not fear the ones who may kill the body, but to Fear (reverently) the One who can kill the body and soul.

Psalms 8:3-6 Man's place in God's plan;

"When I consider your heavens, the work of your fingers, the moon and the stars, which you have ordained; what is man, that you are mindful of him? Or the son of man, that you visited him? You have made him but little lower than the angels, and crowned him with glory and honor. You made him to have dominion over the works of your hands; you have put all things under his feet."

Why is man so important to God? Why does He love us so much that He sent His very Son to die for us? Why? This is an age old question, probably asked at one time or another by every person ever born. In Genesis 1:26 God said to Himself and His council in heaven, "Let Us make man in Our image and after Our likeness." That man, made in the image of God was given a free will and dominion over the earth, which is God's, and over all other created things. This man was a divine spirit being same as God, complete in all ways including the will to choose. We see this in Jesus' discussion with the woman at the well, where He says that God is spirit. He then formed a body out of the dust of the earth, for His newly created spirit being Son. After creating a wonderfully beautiful garden, He placed this man He called Adam, into this garden to tend it. By this act alone, we see

God's tremendous Love for His man. He desired to have a family through this man. Not at all like the angels who are also spirit beings but without the ability to choose and love. God placed His Love inside this man when He breathed the breath of Life into him and caused him to be a living soul.

We all know the rest of the story of how Adam betrayed God by disobeying Him and died spiritually to God's Love and Affection, and became a child of Satan or the god of this world, and merely a man of flesh filled with darkness. God did not give up though, did He? He made the Way for that man to become His son again. That's why this book was written, to show you the mysteries of how to become God's Adam again. Thank God for His Loving Kindness and never ending Mercy.

TRUE PRAISE

T o praise God in the way that is truly meaningful and the way He wants to be praised is this; TO BECOME ONE WITH HIM THROUGH JESUS CHRIST. If you have not spiritually discerned this concept, but are struggling to maintain that emotional high you received at church one night while "revival" was going on, you are not one with Him.

It's a spiritual awakening (for lack of a better term) of the "Seed" which is Jesus, that was planted in mankind when Adam chose to eat the fruit of the tree of the knowledge of good and evil.

When Adam was created in the beginning, God took the dust of the earth (mud) and formed a body. All it did at that time was lay there looking empty, like a manikin in a store display. Then God "breathed" into that body, the breath of life (in the Greek Septuagint LXX that word is BIRTHED) you might then say that God "birthed" life into man.

When we receive Jesus Christ as our Lord and Savior, we actually do more than repeat a rehearsed prayer that someone told us to say. If we have been lead in the TRUTH of the Word, we will have spiritually discerned this reality, otherwise all we do is get very emotional about our being a sinner, having been caught in our sin. It's not to be an emotional thing.

Well, yea we do get emotional just like we do when a child is born into the family. But when the emotional high wears off that child still needs to be cared for through diapering and feeding. This includes all the "dirty" diapers and all the burps and spit ups of feeding. All the middle of the nights having to get up out of our nice warm beds to tend to this helpless child.

Now, here is the funny analogy I got from God this morning which prompted me to ask the question of "How do we truly praise God in the way that pleases Him".

Imagine a couple wanting a child, they must come together so that the mans sperm can be joined with the woman's seed. Correct? Well, that's how it used to be done before science fiction took over!!

Okay, so picture this . . . . the sperm are all gathered together and are no where near that seed in order to cause life to come into it. But, suddenly they all just burst into the loudest roaring of Hallelujahs you ever heard!!! They begin jumping up and down, waving their little tails (remember they're sperm, so they have no hands and arms!) Why are they doing this??? They believe they are praising God! But, God don't require or even desire they do that! He don't? NO!!!

What God desires is for that sperm and seed to come together as one in new life, then for that new life to grow and mature into a being like it's father. So, as we, the lifeless body, come into contact with the One Who gives life and become One with Him, then we grow and mature into the image of the Father WE GIVE HIM PRAISE!!!

The jumping up and down, waving our arms and hands or running with banners and blowing horns was okay for Israel in the Old Testament, but that's not what our Father wants now. No, He wants us to be His children, growing in maturity and knowledge of Him. Every father here on earth wants a son to be just like him, right? Well, most fathers anyway. What makes our Heavenly Father any different? He wants children to be in the image and likeness of their Father, and in order for us to become that, we must become "a spiritual being" just like Him. That's why Jesus, after He ascended to heaven, returned in the form of the Holy Spirit, so that He could lead us and guide us or train us in the way the Father wants us to be. Once we come into that "being" or regeneration, we give Him praise unspeakable and full of Glory.

ACTS 11-

(Gen 2 Restored to Man in Love Grace Faith Joy Life

1 & 2 Thes   1 & 2 Tim   Tit
CHURCH GOVERNMENT

Active in Christ through Christ the Seed
Eph Phil Col
SALVATION

Correction in Situation in Righteousness

HEB. Rom. 1 & 2 Cor Gal
DOCTRINE   REPROOF   SPIRITUAL DEVELOPMENT GROUND
2 Tim   3:16
Act in Christ the Seed

RIGHTEOUSNESS RESTORED TO ALL
RESTORED BY PERSONAL CHOICE

REDEEMED
Acts 1-8
Gen 3:15,21

MAN IS SPIRIT IN A BODY

ALL MAN KIND LOST REDEEMER PROMISED
Gen 3:15,21

RELIGION

LITERAL   MATERIALISTIC

HEBREWS (JEWISH)

Moses

The Voice of man's flesh is heard
The seed of God in man's soul

Flood   Tower of Babel   Abram Called   Moses

NATIONS (Gentiles)

Ps 2:1 →

Adam
Gen 2:7, 21-24

Man
Gen 1:26-27

FIRST BLOOD

Revelation of Christ   12-∞

6 The Voice of man flesh
SIN DEATH
6 man's R
P A 6 man's S
E S T   G O V E R N   N MEAT

1:3
30-Seal
61-70AD
Christian Resurrection

Second Adam
Gen 3:15

Jesus 8 man

John the Baptist Born

Sons of Darkness

Soul of Travail
Dan 9:21-27

ACTS

Paul dead death
Peter 66-0

Christian Age
4-12
∞

8

At this time we would like to share with you a list of some of the books that the Holy Spirit led us to during our wilderness training period. I call it "wilderness" because He took us out to the desert (metaphorically speaking) after we finally understood what He was telling us to do. We used to read almost anything that we could get our hands on but found that only caused confusion. At one point I put my Bible down and told God that I could not do this anymore. It He did not show me what was true Himself, I wasn't having anymore to do with this thing called Christianity. For about 2 years I didn't even know where my Bible was, and I guess that's what God wanted! Because in that time He began moving within both of us individually and as a couple, in a way we never had done before. From that time on, we do not read books or study under any authors that He does not lead us to. It is our prayer that you too, will find your way through some of these materials. Some are hard to grasp at first, because of the language or usage of words. Some people say the authors are heretics, and I'm sure some will say that about us too. It matters not what others think or say but what God says is all that matters.

William Law:
A Demonstration of the Gross and Fundamental Error
A Serious Call to a Devout and Holy Life
Address to the Clergy
Dying to Self
The Grounds and Reasons of Christians Regeneration
The Way to Divine Knowledge

Andrew Murray:
Humility
Inner Chamber
School of Obedience
The Holiest of All
The Power of the Blood
The Prayer Life
Two Covenants

Major William Ian Thomas:
If I Perish I Perish
Saving Life of Christ
The Mystery of Godliness

Charlies G. Trumbull:
The Life that Wins
Victory in Christ

Richard Baxter:
A Call to the Unconverted to Turn
The Causes and Dangers of Slighting Christ and His Gospel

Leo Tolstoy:
The Gospel in Brief*

St. John of the Cross:
Ascent of Mt. Carmel
Dark Night of the Soul

L.E. Maxwell:
Born Crucified

F.B. Meyer:
The Way into the Holiest

James A Fowler, "Christ In You Ministries":
Christ at Work In You
Man As God Intended
Spirit Union Soul Rest
The Four Gospels*
Available at "christinyou.com".

Les Feldick
An online Ministry which has 82 small books of twelve chapters each revealing the basics of Bible Study. Available at "lesfeldick.org".

Additional materials and books can be found at "Christian Classics Ethereal Library" at "www.ccel.org"

---

*   These two books go hand in hand in revealing the kingdom of God restored within the soul of man.

We have alluded through this book about other books to follow. These will only be done as God provides the funds to publish. May God richly bless you in your quest for growth in Him.